NEW DIRECTIONS FOR TEACHING AND LEARNING

Marilla D. Svinicki, *University of Texas, Austin*
EDITOR-IN-CHIEF

R. Eugene Rice, *American Association for Higher Education*
CONSULTING EDITOR

Valuing and Supporting Undergraduate Research

Joyce Kinkead
Utah State University

EDITOR

D1605956

Number 93, Spring 2003

JOSSEY-BASS
San Francisco

VALUING AND SUPPORTING UNDERGRADUATE RESEARCH
Joyce Kinkead (ed.)
New Directions for Teaching and Learning, no. 93
Marilla D. Svinicki, Editor-in-Chief
R. Eugene Rice, Consulting Editor

Microfilm copies of issues and articles are available in 16mm and 35mm, as well as microfiche in 105mm, through University Microfilms Inc., 300 North Zeeb Road, Ann Arbor, Michigan 48106-1346.

ISSN 0271-0633   electronic ISSN 1536-0768

NEW DIRECTIONS FOR TEACHING AND LEARNING is part of The Jossey-Bass Higher and Adult Education Series and is published quarterly by Wiley Subscription Services, Inc., A Wiley Company, at Jossey-Bass, 989 Market Street, San Francisco, California 94103-1741. Periodicals postage paid at San Francisco, California, and at additional mailing offices. Postmaster: Send address changes to New Directions for Teaching and Learning, Jossey-Bass, 989 Market Street, San Francisco, California 94103-1741.

New Directions for Teaching and Learning is indexed in College Student Personnel Abstracts, Contents Pages in Education, and Current Index to Journals in Education (ERIC).

SUBSCRIPTIONS cost $70 for individuals and $145 for institutions, agencies, and libraries. Prices subject to change.

EDITORIAL CORRESPONDENCE should be sent to the editor-in-chief, Marilla D. Svinicki, The Center for Teaching Effectiveness, University of Texas at Austin, Main Building 2200, Austin, TX 78712-1111.

Cover photograph by Richard Blair/Color & Light © 1990.

www.josseybass.com

CONTENTS

About This Publication. Since 1980, *New Directions for Teaching and Learning (NDTL)* has brought a unique blend of theory, research, and practice to leaders in postsecondary education. *NDTL* volumes strive not only for solid substance but also for timeliness, compactness, and accessibility.

The series has four goals: to inform readers about current and future directions in teaching and learning in postsecondary education, to illuminate the context that shapes these new directions, to illustrate these new directions through examples from real settings, and to propose ways in which these new directions can be incorporated into still other settings.

This publication reflects the view that teaching deserves respect as a high form of scholarship. We believe that significant scholarship is conducted not only by researchers who report results of empirical investigations but also by practitioners who share disciplined reflections about teaching. Contributors to *NDTL* approach questions of teaching and learning as seriously as they approach substantive questions in their own disciplines, and they deal not only with pedagogical issues but also with the intellectual and social context in which these issues arise. Authors deal on one hand with theory and research and on the other with practice, and they translate from research and theory to practice and back again.

About This Volume. Undergraduate research is garnering increased attention at various kinds of institutions nationally. Research helps students understand scientific methods, develop skills in problem solving and critical thinking, and work collaboratively with others. The work of undergraduate researchers can also contribute to the institution's goals of furthering knowledge and meeting societal challenges. Students, faculty, and institutions all benefit from the challenges of undergraduate research.

Marilla D. Svinicki
Editor-in-Chief

MARILLA D. SVINICKI is director of the Center for Teaching Effectiveness at the University of Texas at Austin.

EDITOR'S NOTES

Undergraduate research is really about teaching and learning. The academy typically uses the triad mission of teaching, learning, and service to define itself; undergraduate research can and often does cross all of these boundaries. Student research is the application of classroom knowledge and learning, where students do hands-on learning, often in the company of a faculty mentor.

The authors gathered in this volume share a deep belief in the value of undergraduate research. Why do we believe that such activity is essential to a student's intellectual development and growth? Research helps students understand the scientific method as well as methods of investigation in other fields of study. Research helps students develop skills in problem solving, critical thinking, and communication. Because much research is done collaboratively, students also learn how to work in teams. Through research projects, students prepare for further work in graduate school or in a career. The work of undergraduate researchers can contribute to an institution's quest to further knowledge and to help society meet its scientific, technological, environmental, economic, and social challenges. In short, undergraduate research is meaningful for the students, their faculty mentors, the colleges and universities where they work, the communities where they reside, and the world itself.

This volume begins with an overview of undergraduate research. For our purposes, *undergraduate research* is defined broadly to encompass research, scholarship, and creative activity. Such research results in a *product*. Chapter One concludes with a list of initiatives an institution might take on, ranging from low to high investment of resources.

Chapter Two, authored by the director of the Reinvention Center, an outgrowth of the Boyer Commission report, offers a summary of the groundbreaking report and provides an update on how institutions of higher education have responded. Impediments to achieving the report's recommendations abound, but national foundations and agencies are striving to provide incentives to help campuses change the way undergraduates are educated.

In Chapter Three, Carolyn Ash Merkel drills deeper into the research university culture to explore four particular campuses and their histories of developing a culture of undergraduate research. Because this volume is organized to provide insight into the institutional contexts necessary to support undergraduate research, Chapter Four by the 2002 president of the Council on Undergraduate Research explores how undergraduate research can (and should) permeate the campuses of primarily undergraduate institutions. Mitchell R. Malachowski, the chapter's author, brings to bear his experience as a scientist and a proponent of undergraduate research programs. In an earlier tenure as a faculty member at Truman State University in Missouri, he was a leader—along with colleague Michael Nelson—in creating one of the first student celebrations of undergraduate research at the state capitol building.

Although the two-year college campus might seem an unlikely place to find undergraduate research, Jorge A. Perez demonstrates in Chapter Five that for some community colleges, such activity is a natural event. These institutions face many more challenges in implementing undergraduate research than research universities where a culture of discovery and research exists.

David F. Lancy describes in Chapter Six the partnership that a family foundation entered into with the National Conferences on Undergraduate Research to encourage and support interdisciplinary research, an area where there is a gap in funding. Descriptions of the funded projects give a sense of excitement on these campuses where the fellowships have sometimes been the catalyst to institutionalize a research program. In Chapter Seven, Lancy describes his efforts as one faculty member engaged in drawing as many students as possible into the club of researchers through curricular and scholarly projects.

Like Lancy, I thought of myself as a lone scholar working to engage students in research projects with interesting and publishable results. I have coauthored essays with undergraduates, largely as a result of class assignments structured to produce viable publications. As a professor of rhetoric and composition, I felt that designing purposeful, meaningful writing assignments was in the best interests of my students, many of them looking to graduate studies.

My interest in the institutionalization of undergraduate research was spurred by a number of people whom I wish to acknowledge. During an American Council on Education Fellowship, which I held in 1999–2000, I benefited from the experience and advice of George S. Emert, Jay Gogue, and Peter Gerity at Utah State University; Larry Vanderhoef, Patricia Turner, and others at the University of California–Davis; Marlene Ross, Paula Brownlee, and others of the American Council of Education; and my colleagues in the class of 1999–2000. Since then, I have led my own campus in efforts to centralize undergraduate research and enhance existing activities while serving first as associate vice president for research and later as vice provost for undergraduate studies and research. I continue to learn how to do my job better from colleagues, notably Stan L. Albrecht, Kermit L. Hall, Brent C. Miller, David Peak, Noelle Cockett, and Daryl DeWald. Stephanie J. Chambers and Matthew Spencer have served as excellent undergraduate research fellows in the program. Countless other faculty and staff work together to review undergraduate research grant proposals, to organize workshops for students, and to celebrate student achievements through "Posters on the Hill" and "Scholars' Day." I was schooled in accounting practices for research by Lorraine Walker and in institutional review board practices by True Rubal. The Undergraduate Research Program at Utah State University has been supported nobly by the vice president for research and by the student government, which generously endowed a travel fund for undergraduates presenting papers at professional conferences. To enact an undergraduate research program is a complex undertaking. I owe a debt of thanks to the many partners on my own campus who have joined in both concrete and intangible ways in this undertaking. In addition, being informed about the many fine programs that exist at other campuses enriches our work.

Undergraduate research is a passion for those who have contributed to this volume. They have a clear vision of the power of this national movement to improve the way students learn and discover on our many and varied campuses.

Joyce Kinkead
Editor

JOYCE KINKEAD is vice provost for undergraduate studies and research and professor of English at Utah State University in Logan, Utah. Her publications include A Schoolmarm All My Life: Personal Narratives from Early Utah *and* Writing Centers in Contexts: Twelve Case Studies; *she was editor of* The Writing Center Journal *for six years. A number of her students in the humanities have publications arising from classes taken with her.*

1

Undergraduate researchers are involved in learning, and universities can structure programs to support them in a number of ways.

Learning Through Inquiry: An Overview of Undergraduate Research

Joyce Kinkead

While an American Council on Education Fellow, I interviewed several undergraduates involved in research. I spent some time with one in her chemistry laboratory. A former English major, Emily impressed her professor of organic chemistry with the "way she thought and wrote," as he put it, prompting him to invite her onto his research team. As she showed me the beakers under the fume hood that contained the contents of her part of the project, Emily said, "You know, in science classes with labs, the experiments always turn out right, but when you're working on your own project, there is a lot of failure. Like the time I stayed all night in the lab, setting the alarm clock for every four hours to check on results. It was the first of a series of such around-the-clock observations. I'm just so much more motivated and interested to see what happens when it's my project."

Emily's undergraduate research story is slightly different from Matt's. Currently an instructor at a two-year college, Matt wrote to me with pride about a graduate school experience: "When I was taking graduate classes back East, I found the professor had assigned an essay that I'd written as an undergraduate in our tutoring seminar—an essay that had been published in a scholarly journal. Did that make me feel like something special!"

Matt and Emily—although humanist and scientist, respectively—share an enthusiasm for hands-on learning that extends classroom knowledge to scholarly application.

NEW DIRECTIONS FOR TEACHING AND LEARNING, no. 93, Spring 2003   © Wiley Periodicals, Inc.

What Is Undergraduate Research?

When I first began my inquiry into undergraduate research and undergraduate research programs, I had several misconceptions. One was that undergraduate research focused on the scientific method. Certainly efforts to enhance instruction in science, mathematics, and engineering have become more vigorous (National Research Council, 1999; National Science Foundation, 1996) because of alarming reports that the United States is falling behind other countries in these areas. Another misperception was that undergraduate research took place outside the regular curriculum. Matt corrected that notion for me by drawing my attention to his scholarly publication, an essay developed within the framework of a seminar.

For our purposes here, *undergraduate research* is defined broadly to include scientific inquiry, creative activity, and scholarship. An undergraduate research project might result in a musical composition, a work of art, an agricultural field experiment, or an analysis of historical documents. The key is that the project produces some original work. Many college and university classes require students to write research papers—too often not requiring original thought and original output. Although Matt's essay was written to meet course requirements, it was sufficiently innovative to be accepted for publication in a peer-reviewed journal. Original work may occur in the context of a class, but it is more likely to occur as an extracurricular activity.

Another hallmark of undergraduate research is the role of the mentor, a faculty member who guides the novice researcher and initiates the student into the methods of a discipline. In Emily's case, she works collaboratively with a faculty member on a faculty-determined project and is responsible for a piece of the greater project. A student might also work as a research assistant to a faculty member, not as a gofer whose responsibilities end at washing test tubes and beakers but as someone learning discrete skills and advancing to more complex tasks. Or an undergraduate researcher might work alone on a self-selected project, meeting regularly with a faculty mentor. Given the range of disciplines in a university campus—science, engineering, humanities, social sciences, and arts—undergraduate research is definitely not a case of "one size fits all." Disciplines also vary in their values. Although some fields place prime value on sole authorship (for example, literary studies), which calls to mind the writer in the garret, other fields (for example, social sciences, science) esteem collaborative work that draws together teams. For the latter kind of endeavor, first authorship is prized, in contrast to sole authorship. The various values, then, create some of the many hurdles a college or university must vault to institutionalize undergraduate research. Faculty members might turn to Merkel's *How to Mentor Undergraduate Researchers* (2002) for guidance.

The Undergraduate Research Imperative

Although research has no doubt been a part of many students' undergraduate careers, a growing movement transcends institutional boundaries and types to produce programmatic undergraduate research initiatives. Universities such as the Massachusetts Institute of Technology or the California Institute of Technology have a fine tradition of such research programs; it is more surprising to find such programs taking root at Truman State University in Missouri or at two-year colleges such as Rockland County Community College in Suffern, New York, and LaGuardia Community College in Long Island City. What factors instigated the broad-based appeal of undergraduate research?

The scientific community, appalled by the number of reports proclaiming the scientific illiteracy of American students, embarked on a national campaign to ground instruction in science and mathematics. One result at the secondary school level was the formation of magnet schools in which students showing an aptitude for science and mathematics received concentrated instruction. Universities have also developed summer academies to focus on the research experience or offer research-based experiences during the regular term. At Utah State University in Logan, ambitious high school students participate in a biology laboratory as part of a school-to-work program to sample what it means to be a scientist. In teacher education programs, students increasingly experience the process of discovery, a process not limited, by the way, to the sciences but extending to such fields as literary studies.

Various reports, especially those of the National Science Foundation (NSF), analyzed and provided strategic vision for improving America's academic future. NSF released its own strategic plan in 1995, a year after the National Science Board published its joint report, *Stresses on Research and Education at Colleges and Universities*. For NSF, three goals were established: enable the United States to uphold a position of world leadership in all aspects of science, mathematics, and engineering; promote the discovery, integration, dissemination, and employment of new knowledge in service to society; and achieve excellence in U.S. science, mathematics, engineering, and technology education at all levels. NSF put theory into practice by funding such programs as Project Kaleidoscope, initiated in 1993 with conversations at the National Academy of Sciences. The project's goals included defining "the dimensions of a research-rich environment and how that environment might be adapted to different academic settings." It also sponsored a convocation focusing on "Shaping the Future," another initiative to reform undergraduate curriculum.

Not since the late 1950s when the United States responded to the "Sputnik challenge" has instruction in science and mathematics received such a shot in the arm. In fact, such instruction had languished. One of the first wake-up calls was the Neal Report (1986), which documented the paltry funds provided to educational initiatives by NSF (National Science Foundation, 1996, p. 1). Creating a panoply of programs to redress the problem, NSF funded curricular reform and research experiences for undergraduates. In addition, to motivate institutions to instigate broad-based programs where students from all disciplines increase their scientific literacy, NSF created recognition awards for the integration of research and education—RAIRE and AIRE prizes—the first set going to ten outstanding research universities and the second to notable primarily undergraduate institutions. Each $500,000 grant funded the expansion of existing programs, the documentation of institutional efforts, and dissemination of those efforts.

At the same time that these forward-looking initiatives were being developed, the media and others called into question the role of research universities and what they viewed as a failure to provide a quality education, especially to baccalaureate-seeking students. While research universities pursued Carnegie Research I designation, focusing on research dollars and graduate students, undergraduates seemed to be increasingly left to teaching assistants, adjuncts, and part-time instructors. Books such as *ProfScam: Professors and the Demise of Higher Education* (Sykes, 1989) revealed the dismal state of higher education to students and their parents, already confused and frustrated by spiraling tuition costs at brand-name institutions that seemed to have abrogated their duty to freshmen and sophomores. The *New York Times* (Richardson, 1995) noted the formation of a panel to investigate the mission of the research university. It was, in fact, a bellwether moment for higher education. The Boyer Report (1998), as *Reinventing Undergraduate Education: A Blueprint for America's Research Universities* came to be called in honor of the late Ernest Boyer, called for "significant transformations" in the way research campuses educate their students. Those transformations include making research-based learning the standard; constructing an inquiry-based freshman year, culminating with a capstone experience; removing barriers to interdisciplinary education; changing faculty reward systems; and cultivating a sense of community. Commissioned by the Carnegie Foundation, the report provides advice for restructuring the entire university, noting that students in research universities often do not reap the benefits of attending such an institution. "Learning is based on discovery guided by mentoring," they note, but more often than not, students find themselves just another seatholder in large-enrollment lecture courses, too anonymous to ever think of asking the professor for a letter of recommendation. Students pay for class notes from a student union counter, opting not to attend class at all except for examinations.

This type of "education," derided by the Boyer Commission, operates from a sage-on-the-stage model, with the students as empty vessels to be filled with knowledge. It does nothing to improve desired workforce skills of communication, collaboration, critical thinking, and problem solving. In contrast, the undergraduate research experience gets at the heart of these skills by providing careful guidance by a mentor faculty member into the inquiry methods of a discipline. Although undergraduate research is not a panacea for all problems, it is acknowledged as one way for students to feel more connected to their educational experience, a practice touted in an earlier Carnegie report, *Involvement in Learning* (National Institute of Education, 1984). Such connected learning has been a hallmark of improved retention rates, too. For these reasons, NSF noted that the most probable audiences for undergraduate research and education initiatives are, first, honors programs but, second, at-risk populations, followed by preservice teachers. Several programs exist—McNair Scholars and CAMP (California Alliance for Minority Participation in Sciences, Engineering, and Mathematics)—to initiate students into research careers. Likewise, initiatives to increase the number of women in the sciences have found improved success rates with an inquiry-based curriculum as opposed to a traditional lecture format.

Recommendations from the Boyer Report draw on the culmination of two decades of pedagogical experimentation in which active learning, student-centered learning, and collaborative learning have become watchwords. Rather than the sage on the stage, faculty members are encouraged to become "guides on the side." These approaches are reinforced by the popular problem-based-learning (PBL) movement housed at Samford University (Birmingham, Alabama) and funded by the Pew Charitable Trust. Originally used in medical schools, PBL is an approach that draws on students' prior knowledge to address and solve knotty discipline-based problems while working in a team in a classroom setting. The Hewlett Foundation sees this as one way that research universities can reform general education to include more interactive learning and so has funded a number of PBL initiatives. John Gardner's work on the first-year experience also contributes to the growing realization that attention must be paid to the critical early years of the baccalaureate (Upcraft, Gardner, and Barefoot, 2003). First-year seminars, freshman-interest groups, linked classes, block scheduling, and the learning-living-residence experiences (Schroeder and Mable, 1994) all draw on the urgent need to address this group of students in the first, formative year of instruction and to build them into a community of learners. The community concept is especially important in large, anonymous research universities where students have a tendency to feel lost and perhaps engage in less positive or even self-destructive behaviors. Leaders in student services, for instance, see the necessity to create co-curricular or extracurricular activities that foster an atmosphere of "work hard, play well."

The heritage of undergraduate research derives significantly from faculty enterprise and effort rather than from institutional movement. Faculty members, intellectually stimulated by their own research and intrinsically interested in their own students' development, have been largely responsible for driving undergraduate research. On some campuses, undergraduate research exists as islands of excellence, whereas on others, ownership of the enterprise has been taken over centrally. The increasing number of a new position—a central administrator dedicated to undergraduate initiatives—is indicative of the attention being paid to these issues. The value of centralization became even more apparent when institutions received the substantial NSF RAIRE or AIRE prizes. By offering monetary rewards—this prize or in grant money itself to support summer fellowships, for instance—NSF is changing the undergraduate landscape and fulfilling its goals as set forth in its strategic plan for the future (1995).

NSF, in fact, defines best practices through its "key factors characteristic of successful programs that integrate research and education": strong institutional support; commitment of faculty and program coordinators; collaborations across disciplines; integration of faculty and student research; student focus, especially to ensure solid training, good advising, and mentoring; undergraduate research opportunities that are visible, provide support, and offer a means of showcasing the products; IBL; external support from donors, grants, foundations, and agencies; professional societies offering vocal support of the integration of research and education; assessment that monitors and evaluates the experiences; and teacher preparation that ensures that the next generation of K-12 teachers will be knowledgeable and able to integrate science in instruction (Proceedings of RAIRE and AIRE Project Directors' Meeting, 1999). In defining these key factors, NSF in effect sets the agenda for higher education—at least those institutions that strive to move forward.

Although some research universities have been notoriously lax in capitalizing on their natural advantages to enhance undergraduate education, one type of institution has consistently participated in undergraduate research: the small, private liberal arts college. A special subset of the PUIs, these colleges justify relatively high tuition and fees through the individualized attention paid to students by the faculty. Undergraduate research projects can provide students with the coinage of the realm that ensures their admittance into prestigious graduate schools. Their portfolios include more than grade-point averages and Graduate Record Examination scores; they may have participated in professional society meetings by delivering papers or making poster presentations, served as coauthors on scholarly articles, or attended a Council on Undergraduate Research (CUR) meeting or one of the National Conferences on Undergraduate Research (NCUR). Such hands-on applications of learning mean an increased likelihood of graduate fellowships or assistantships. When John Strassburger notes in his "Embracing Undergraduate Research" (1995) that undergraduate research is a "national trend," he draws on his experience as president at two small liberal arts colleges. He notes of Ursinus College in Collegeville, Pennsylvania, that the "overwhelming majority of all psychology majors participate in undergraduate research, many of them ending up as coauthors on professional papers" (p. 3). For these students, undergraduate research is an "expectation in department after department."

Target Candidates for Undergraduate Research

Honors programs—units that seek to provide the best educational opportunities to the cream of the student population—are natural sites for undergraduate research. An honors program may have its own funding to support
undergraduate projects. Such competitive grant programs range from a few
hundred to several thousand dollars. Honors students are more likely to
know and to feel comfortable with potential faculty mentors, whom they
may have met in the seminar-sized honors-designated courses. These students also plan for graduate school careers and are prepared to be as attractive as possible for financial support from their schools of choice. The
honors student, then, is a natural for undergraduate research. Research project experience is also crucial to premedical students who must acquire solid
letters of reference and demonstrate discovery experience.

A second prospective candidate for undergraduate research is the student defined as at risk or underrepresented in a field of study. At what some
might see as the opposite end of the continuum from honors students, at-
risk students benefit from the same advantages offered by undergraduate
research. They engage in a meaningful project with a faculty mentor committed to intellectual discovery. In essence, they gain an understanding early
about the heart of the academic enterprise. The University of Michigan
notes the increased retention especially of African-American men who
engage in research projects during year one (Nagda and others, 1998).
Because this special population of students may not have come from academically advantaged elementary and secondary schools, it is especially
important that programs targeted at them include cognitive and skill development, structuring the experience for continued growth and increasing
independence. Such programs are often highly structured, with successful
upper-class students serving as peer mentors in addition to graduate student and faculty mentors. Students may receive assistance in writing
abstracts for professional presentations and preparing posters or papers.
Modeling the way researchers behave is an important part of such programs.
Proponents of specialized programs cite the paucity of women and ethnic
students seeking careers in science and technology. They also note that it is
economically wise to diversify these fields and prepare students for such
careers where they may serve as role models for future students—who are
predicted to no longer be "minority" but "majority" students.

The third target group for undergraduate research, preservice teachers, derives from the initiative to change K-12 education to incorporate discovery learning at all levels. Research universities have typically shied away
from teacher education programs, the effect of an elitist—almost snob-
bish—attitude that, given the low salaries, the best students do not seek
careers as elementary and high school teachers. Universities have preferred
to focus instead on students who are geared to careers in government,
industry, the corporate world, or higher education. A strong mandate exists
for institutions that are outstanding in science education and research to

join in solving what has become a national crisis (well described in the American Council on Education's report *To Touch the Future: Transforming the Way Teachers Are Taught,* 1999). Just as undergraduates can become more engaged and motivated by participating in the scientific method, so can much younger students. Colleges and universities have a vested interest in supporting and promoting improved K-12 education because students with solid academic training can begin at college levels and avoid expensive remedial instruction.

Although in this section of the chapter I have focused largely on science, technology, engineering, and mathematics (frequently abbreviated to the STEM programs), undergraduate research is by no means limited to these areas. A student is just as likely to undertake an investigation into a subject in the classics or linguistics as in biology or mathematics.

Administration of Undergraduate Research Programs

When I mentioned to a university president that undergraduate research might be housed in a variety of places on campus, he contradicted me, adamant that undergraduate research is a teaching activity and thus rightly belongs under the auspices of the chief academic officer. On the other hand, if funding to support the program is derived from the office of research, then the administrator responsible for funding may wish the program housed in that office; in fact, a number of undergraduate research programs are overseen by the institutional research office. In my own case as vice provost of undergraduate studies and research, I am housed in the office of the provost, but the research office pays a portion of my salary. I attend staff meetings of both the provost and the vice president of research, serving as a link between the two offices. The vice president of research provides funding for most of our undergraduate research activity, although the student government offers a travel fund to support undergraduate research presentation of projects at professional conferences.

On some campuses, the undergraduate research is housed in the honors program. Although this may be convenient to students receiving presidential scholarships and who are naturally likely participants in discovery and inquiry, this administrative home may send the wrong message to students who feel shut out if they are not honors students.

Funding and Resources to Support Undergraduate Research

Logically, returned overhead monies generated through faculty research activities could be a prime source of support for undergraduates engaged in research. Because some institutions see inquiry as a teaching-learning activity, the funding might legitimately be a line item, supported by education and general allocations from the state. At private institutions, a program may be endowed, and in fact, some are generously endowed to the tune of many millions of dollars (for example, California Institute of Technology and Cornell University, Ithaca, New York). Mark C. Zrull of Appalachian State University (Boone, North Carolina) may have hit on the most imaginative source of funding when he won agreement from the business office to use money spent at the student laundries to support undergraduate research activities (Zrull, 2002).

What is funding used for? For centralized programs, administrative oversight is necessary and may be part of the undergraduate education administrator's purview. That person will require clerical help and assistance with programs. Student grants, fellowships, stipends for faculty mentors, travel funds, materials, scholarships, and awards can require a substantial budget. A central administrator responsible for undergraduate research will naturally be alert to fundraising opportunities from either private sources or agencies. In some cases, federal work-study funds may be garnered for support of undergraduate researchers. For other students, academic credit may suffice.

Celebrating Undergraduate Research

For many students and faculty, the act of research and its resulting product is reward enough; however, public recognition is important. The importance of written policy statements that take into account the mentoring of undergraduates as part of the faculty role and reward cannot be underestimated. The lack of concrete recognition of this valuable work can be a stumbling block to institutionalizing undergraduate research. An annual celebration as a culmination of the academic year provides a venue for showcasing students and faculty. At Utah State University, April is designated as Undergraduate Research Month, and scheduled events include readings of creative writers, art shows, research posters, faculty honors lectures, workshops on research ethics, and awards.

Student research products are disseminated at professional societies and associations, the biennial Council on Undergraduate Research, the annual NCUR, CUR's Washington, D.C.-based "Posters on the Hill," research days at the state capital, and electronic and print journals. The National Undergraduate Research Clearinghouse (http://clearinghouse. mwsc.edu), which is funded by an NSF grant and housed at Missouri Western State College in St. Joseph, exists to disseminate student research and to increase access to research in a variety of scientific disciplines.

Ethical Considerations for Undergraduate Researchers

For faculty and student researchers alike, ethical considerations for conducting research are in the spotlight, driven by public outrage over research projects that misfired and resulted in the death of human subjects. When my colleague Bruce Bugbee won our campus's Graduate Mentor of the Year Award, he used the prize money to purchase for faculty and students copies of *On Being a Scientist* (Committee on Science, Engineering, and Public Policy, 1995), a publication that answers questions such as when is it ethical to throw out bad data? When is it a conflict of interest? What is misconduct in science? The chapters are illustrated with useful case studies so that the guide can be used in classes, at club meetings, and at orientations. Students can and often do become acquainted with the ethics of doing research early in the undergraduate career, typically in a university writing program where issues of academic honesty are discussed. Any research writing course can take on the larger task of introducing the principles of responsible conduct, but faculty responsible for the oversight of writing programs may need to be informed about the larger service they provide the institution by integrating discussions on academic integrity. At Utah State University, we have revised our sophomore-level research writing course to integrate information about undergraduate research opportunities and responsible conduct in research as well as practice in writing sample proposals and presenting results of research papers. In addition, we sponsor an "Integrity Matters" Week to focus on a diverse range of ethical topics: human subject research, the use of animals in research, fund-accounting principles, plagiarism, fabrication, and authorship.

Questions to Ask About Institutionalizing Undergraduate Research

No one model describes all undergraduate research programs. An institution that is investigating establishing or enhancing undergraduate research has a number of options.

Description of the undergraduate research program. Is it targeted at lower-division only? Upper-division only? Summer research fellowships? What are the participation rates? What are the relevant data? How and when did the program begin?

Administrative oversight and organization. Is the program housed with the chief academic officer? The honors program? The office for research? What are the reporting lines? How are policies established and implemented? Does the program function as a central clearinghouse, or is it more decentralized?

Funding, resources, and sources of funds. Is the program a line item? Is it funded via grants, overhead, and contracts or endowments? What is the level of support for student stipends, grants, travel, and internships? Are scholarships designated in such a way that participation as an undergraduate researcher is an expectation? Is there a faculty grant program?

Description of student research, including possibilities for creative, scholarly, and research activities.

Ways and means of disseminating and showcasing student work. Is there a student research journal, print or electronic? Do students attend professional meetings? Is there support for publication? Is there support for CUR or NCUR attendance? Do students participate in CUR's initiative on "Posters on the Hill" for legislators? Is there an on-campus student research symposium?

Special programs for targeted populations such as preservice teachers, honors students, at-risk students, and underrepresented students.

Ideas for initiating activities in nonscience areas and interdisciplinary research. Nationally, the humanities have been considered difficult for undergraduate scholars to find opportunities.

Faculty rewards and incentives.

Integration of research into the curriculum. Are courses sequenced for increasingly complex tasks, beginning with an IBL foundation?

Intersections between undergraduate research and other units of the campus. Is community-action research—that is, undergraduate research meets service learning—a component? Does an institution-specific mission such as a "land grant" influence undergraduate research so that it has an outreach flavor? Or is it part of a cooperative extension? Are housing units designated for undergraduate researchers?

Assessment of undergraduate research. What are the data that show that such programs make a difference and do indeed add value? (The University of Delaware, led by Joan Bennett, director of its program, has produced a number of assessment reports, many of them available on the program's Web site [http://www.udel.edu/UR].)

Challenges that have faced the program.

Other strengths of the program. For instance, has the institutional public relations staff made use of the undergraduate research program to market the university?

How will the institution initiate students into the responsible conduct of research?

Resources

CUR publishes in its "How To" series many guides for faculty and administrators. Especially noteworthy is Toufic Hakim's *How to Develop and Administer Institutional Research Programs* (2000). In meeting its mission to "support and promote high-quality undergraduate student-faculty collaborative research and scholarship," CUR also sponsors workshops for faculty. The *CUR Quarterly* provides useful articles, news, and announcements. Information about CUR programs and publications is available on its Web site: http://www.cur.org.

CUR was originally founded to promote scientific research by undergraduates at PUIs. NCUR, established some years later, broadened its mandate to be inclusive of all fields of study. Its annual conference, held each spring, attracts nearly two thousand students and faculty (Web site: http://www.ncur.org).

Project Kaleidoscope, funded by NSF, seeks to improve teaching and learning in sciences, technology, engineering, and mathematics. Information on its summer conferences and the network of faculty engaged in this work can be obtained on its Web site (http://www.pkal.org).

Preparatory work to undergraduate work may involve IBL courses. Many of these take problem-based learning as a method, and Samford University houses the Pew-funded problem-based learning initiative (http://www.samford.edu/pbl).

The Reinvention Center at SUNY–Stony Brook has undertaken the task of creating a resources page at its Web site (http://www.sunysb.edu/reinvent) and updates it frequently, including links to universities with undergraduate research programs. The center sponsors regional network meetings and in November 2002 organized a national meeting that focused on undergraduate education—and research in particular—at the research university.

As undergraduate research extends its reach, those interested in learning more can find a growing number of publications, testament to the increasing emphasis placed on hands-on research learning for students. Only a few years ago, a paucity of information was available, but spurred by CUR, NCUR, and the Boyer Commission, that gap is being filled.

References

American Council on Education (ACE) Presidents' Task Force Report on Teacher Education. *To Touch the Future: Transforming the Way Teachers Are Taught.* Washington, D.C.: American Council on Education, 1999.

Boyer Commission on Educating Undergraduates in the Research University, S. S. Kenny (chair). *Reinventing Undergraduate Education: A Blueprint for America's Research Universities.* State University of New York-Stony Brook, 1998.

Committee on Science, Engineering, and Public Policy, National Academy of Engineering, Institute of Medicine, National Academy of Sciences. *On Being a Scientist: Responsible Conduct in Research.* Washington, D.C.: National Academy Press, 1995.

Hakim, T. *How to Develop and Administer Institutional Research Programs.* Washington, D.C.: Council on Undergraduate Research, 2000.

Merkel, C. A. *How to Mentor Undergraduate Researchers.* Washington, D.C.: Council on Undergraduate Research, 2002.

Nagda, B. A., and others. "Undergraduate Student-Faculty Research Partnerships Affect Student Retention." *Review of Higher Education,* 1998, 22(1), 55–62.

National Institute of Education. *Involvement in Learning: Realizing the Potential of Higher Education.* Washington, D.C.: National Institute of Education, 1984.

National Research Council. *Transforming Undergraduate Education in Science, Mathematics, Engineering, and Technology.* Washington, D.C.: National Science Foundation, 1999.

National Science Board, Task Committee on Undergraduate Science and Engineering Education, H. A. Neal (chair). *Undergraduate Science, Mathematics and Engineering Education; Role for the National Science Foundation and Recommendations for Action by Other Sectors to Strengthen Collegiate Education and Pursue Excellence in the Next*

Generation of U.S. Leadership in Science and Technology. National Science Foundation publication no. NSB 86–100. Washington, D.C.: National Science Foundation, 1986.

National Science Board and Government-University-Industry Research Roundtable. *Stresses on Research and Education at Colleges and Universities: Institutional and Sponsoring Agency Responses.* Joint Report. Washington, D.C.: National Research Council, 1994.

National Science Foundation. *NSF in a Changing World: The National Science Foundation's Strategic Plan.* Washington, D.C.: National Science Foundation, 1995.

National Science Foundation. *Shaping the Future: New Expectations for Undergraduate Education in Science, Mathematics, Engineering, and Technology.* National Science Foundation publication no. 96–139. Washington, D.C.: National Science Foundation, 1996.

Richardson, L. "Academic Panel to Ponder the Mission of Research Universities." *New York Times,* May 3, 1995, p. B9.

Schroeder, C., and Mable, P. *Realizing the Educational Potential of Residence Halls.* San Francisco: Jossey-Bass, 1994.

Strassburger, J. "Embracing Undergraduate Research." *AAHE Bulletin,* 1995, 47, 3–5.

Sykes, C. J. *ProfScam: Professors and the Demise of Higher Education.* New York: St. Martin's, 1989.

Upcraft, M. L., Gardner, J. N., and Barefoot, B. O. *The First Year Student: Understanding, Teaching, and Supporting.* San Francicsco: Jossey-Bass, 2003.

Zrull, M. "Undergraduate Research Programs: Different Approaches to Reaching the Same Goal." Presentation at the Council on Undergraduate Research National Conference, June 2002.

JOYCE KINKEAD is vice provost for undergraduate studies and research and professor of English at Utah State University in Logan.

2

Spurred by the Boyer Report, research universities have made considerable progress in raising the status of undergraduate education and transforming it in ways that bring inquiry to the fore.

The Boyer Commission Report and Its Impact on Undergraduate Research

Wendy Katkin

When the Boyer Commission on Educating Undergraduates in the Research University was formed in 1995, numerous surveys and studies were already questioning aspects of undergraduate education in the United States and calling for examination of some of its underlying assumptions. These studies typically were driven by current and projected demographic, economic, and technological changes in this country. In addition, academic and government officials and leaders in the private sector were concerned that our colleges and universities were producing baccalaureate graduates who were ill prepared for both the current workforce and the new and emerging demands of the twenty-first century. A related issue was the decline of U.S. citizens who were majoring in mathematics, science, and technological disciplines and the low female and minority representation in these disciplines. Between 1985 and 1995, groups as varied as the American Council on Education, Sigma Xi, National Research Council, National Endowment for the Humanities, National Science Foundation, and National Association of Colleges and Employers held conferences and issued reports that focused attention on specific problems and shortcomings and advocated change. At stake, it was argued, was the U.S.'s economic and technological competitiveness.

The work that perhaps more than any other stimulated the discussion was *A Nation at Risk* (National Commission on Excellence in Education, 1983). Although concerned primarily with grades K-12, *A Nation at Risk* nevertheless served as a wake-up call for higher education as well. Among the most influential studies with a higher education focus to follow its publication were *Undergraduate Science, Mathematics, and Engineering Education* (National Science Board, Vol. 1, 1986); *College: The Undergraduate*

Experience in America (Boyer, 1987); *Educating One-Third of a Nation* (American Council on Education, 1988); *50 Hours: A Core Curriculum for College Students* (Cheney, 1989); *Universities, and the Future of America* (Bok, 1990); *Scholarship Reconsidered: Priorities of the Professoriate* (Boyer, 1990); *Investing in Human Potential: Science and Engineering at the Crossroads* (Matyas and Malcolm, 1991); *Gaining the Competitive Edge* (National Science Foundation, 1993); and *Talking About Leaving: Factors Contributing to High Attrition Rates Among Science, Mathematics, and Engineering Undergraduate Majors* (Seymour and Hewitt, 1994). Although each of these publications had its own focus and target audience, they shared a common recognition that the traditions and practices that had shaped undergraduate education in the past no longer sufficed. Change would require new and innovative modes of teaching and learning that took into account the changing state of knowledge and expanding curricular needs, faculty pressures, and an increasingly diverse undergraduate population. A 1989 conference, "An Exploration of the Nature and Quality of Undergraduate Education in Science, Mathematics, and Engineering," sponsored by Sigma Xi and supported by the National Science Foundation and the Johnson Foundation, captured the essence of the national debate. The goal of the conference was "to identify fundamental topics and issues that should be addressed in charting policy for undergraduate education in science, mathematics, and engineering" (Sigma Xi, 1989, www.sigmaxi.org).

Collectively, the various reports and national forums generated considerable discussion and debate in the higher education community, and they led to significant reform efforts on many campuses. The four-year liberal arts colleges were perhaps the most aggressive in responding, both with curricular and pedagogical experimentation on their own campuses and through combined action. Organizations such as the Council on Undergraduate Research, which had been in existence since 1978, and Project Kaleidoscope (PKAL), founded in 1989, led the effort. PKAL's "driving goals" were "to equip teams of faculty and administrators for leadership in reform at the local level, so that students and science are better served, as well as to encourage broad understanding of how strong undergraduate STEM [science, technology, engineering, and mathematics] programs serve the national interest" (http://www.pkal.org). Its approach has been to identify successful programs and practices, bring them to the attention of the larger undergraduate educational community, and facilitate their adaptation in other settings.

In contrast, the response of research universities was for the most part slow, scattered, and largely at the margins—"cosmetic surgery" as the Boyer Commission called it (1998, p. 6). Their response was often based on the blind acceptance of models that had proved successful at four-year colleges but did not readily translate to research universities. Often there was no meaningful consideration of the unique "ecosystem" and singular attributes of the research university itself. Yet, such consideration is essential to transformation.

The National Commission on Educating Undergraduates in the Research University (hereafter referred to as the Boyer Commission), made up of eminent and creative thinkers from academia, government, and the arts, was formed during this period of academic ferment. It was created under the auspices of the Carnegie Foundation for the Advancement of Teaching. The foundation's president, Ernest L. Boyer, presided at its first meeting in July 1995. When Boyer died five months later, in December, the commission was renamed in his memory. From the outset, the Boyer Commission differed in two significant ways from other groups examining undergraduate education: its exclusive emphasis on research universities and its determination to offer a blueprint, a vision—along with a delineation of the ways to achieve it—that would serve as a guide for transformation.

Emphasis on Research Universities

In virtually all of the prior reports, undergraduate education had been considered globally, without differentiating among the distinctive characteristics of the diverse institutions that offer this education and the distinctive challenges and opportunities they each afford. The commission departed from this practice for two important reasons.

The first related to the sheer number of undergraduates research universities serve. Although research universities represent only 3 percent of institutions within higher education, they typically confer 32 percent of all baccalaureate degrees awarded annually in the United States and 56 percent of the baccalaureate degrees earned by recent recipients of science and engineering doctorates (Boyer Commission, 1998, p. 5). "To an overwhelming degree, they have furnished the cultural, intellectual, economic, and political leadership of the nation" (Boyer Commission, 1998, p. 5). At the same time, by giving students "too little that will be of real value beyond a credential that will help them get their first jobs" (Boyer Commission, 1998, p. 6), too often, research universities were "shortchanging" their students (Boyer Commission, 1998, p. 5). This shortchanging derived from several factors, most notably the prevalence of models of teaching and learning that fail to engage students, enable them to make connections across spheres of knowledge, or enhance their development of critical skills.

The second factor underlying the commission's exclusive focus was its recognition that research universities are markedly different from four-year liberal arts colleges and other institutions of higher education. Furthermore, they have the potential to offer a significantly different and rich undergraduate experience based on their unique missions and assets: "research universities share a special set of characteristics and experience a range of common challenges in relation to their undergraduate students" (Boyer Commission, 1998, p. 1). Among their most noteworthy characteristics are their multiple missions; the high number and wide range of baccalaureate and doctoral degrees they offer; a defining commitment to creating knowledge, which shapes the faculty's values and activities; the presence of graduate students; and enormous diversity within the university community population. The challenge, commission members argued, is for research universities to bring these elements to bear on the undergraduate education they provide and to create a model that draws on the mode of inquiry that is fundamental to their research and scholarly activities and their training of graduate students.

> What is needed now is a new model of undergraduate education at research universities that makes the baccalaureate experience an inseparable part of an integrated whole. Universities need to take advantage of the immense resources of their graduate and research programs to strengthen the quality of undergraduate education, rather than striving to replicate the special environment of the liberal arts college. There needs to be a symbiotic relationship between all the participants in university learning that will provide a new kind of undergraduate experience available only at research universities. Moreover, productive research faculties might find new stimulation and new creativity in contact with bright, imaginative and eager baccalaureate students, and graduate students would benefit from integrating their research and teaching experiences. Research universities are distinctly different from small colleges, and they need to offer an experience that is a clear alternative to the college experience [Boyer Commission, 1998, pp. 7–8].

In adopting this approach, the commission took its cue from Boyer: "the most important obligation now confronting the nation's colleges and universities is to break out of the tired old teaching versus research debate and define, in more creative ways, what it means to be a scholar" (Boyer, 1990, p. xii).

The Boyer Commission Blueprint

The Boyer Commission also differed from previous groups in its call for action and its provision of a prescription, as it were, based on research universities' unique characteristics and differences. In its report, the Boyer Commission offered ten specific recommendations to address deficiencies in the current undergraduate education provided at research universities and to help institutions use their singular strengths and resources to go to the next step, to initiate activities that would lead ultimately to the kind of educational transformation advocated by the commission members.

The title of its report, *Reinventing Undergraduate Education: A Blueprint for America's Research Universities,* conveyed clearly the Boyer Commission's highly focused and powerful message, as well as its confidence that the desired change could and would be achieved if specific actions were undertaken. Perhaps because of the challenge it posed to traditional modes, the report generated considerable discussion and controversy. Although many applauded its frankness and freshness and its concrete recommendations, others argued that the recommendations were impractical, expensive, and unrealistic in light of the research university's complex culture; the demands on faculty; and the large, diverse populations research universities serve. A number of academicians criticized the report's failure to note the considerable progress that had been made in recent years to elevate the status of teaching and make research universities friendlier. Others questioned whether the report would have any effect.

In an article in the *Chronicle of Higher Education,* Robin Wilson presented two prevailing perspectives on the report's potential effects (1998). Arthur E. Levine, president of Teachers College at Columbia University, suggested that "Institutions are having a harder time placing PhD recipients in academic jobs and are being forced to pay more attention to the real bread and butter—undergraduates. . . . If research universities hope to maintain their enrollments, they have to offer programs that respond to undergraduates in more congenial environments. . . . Perhaps this is not a bad time to issue a report" (Wilson, 1998, p. A13). Ted Marchese, vice president of the American Association for Higher Education, disagreed: "Conditions have improved for universities. . . . The net result is that the perceived pressures to do something fundamentally better with undergraduates have lessened a bit" (Wilson, 1998, p. A13). Shirley Strum Kenny, president of the State University of New York at Stony Brook and Boyer's successor as chair of the commission, expressed a cautious optimism: whereas universities "have done a lot of interesting things [to fix the problem of undergraduate education]. . . . these things never became part of the real value system of research universities and it's really time to do something about it." Her hope was that the report would at least "shape the debate" on the subject (Wilson, 1998, p. 12).

Who was right? In 2001, at the request of the Boyer Commission, the Reinvention Center at Stony Brook, which was established in 2000 as an outgrowth of the Boyer Commission, undertook a survey to determine the extent to which research universities had incorporated elements of the commission's recommendations (Boyer Commission, 2002). Of the 123 research universities that offer baccalaureate degree programs, ninety-one (74 percent) responded. In addition, Reinvention Center staff conducted lengthy follow-up interviews with academic administrators at forty of these institutions and used a subset of survey items as the focus of discussions at regional network meetings sponsored by the center and attended by about two hundred faculty and administrators. The purpose of the interviews and the discussions was to develop a more complete picture of changes that may have taken place in undergraduate education at research universities, particularly with reference to the Boyer Commission recommendations, than data alone could yield. The faculty's input at the meetings was particularly important in achieving a balanced perspective.

Interestingly, the survey and follow-up activities revealed that few campuses have systematically collected data that would yield the answers. Most do not know, for example, exactly how many of their undergraduates are involved in research or scholarship, how many faculty supervise them, or the proportion of their students who do senior projects. Most of the responses to the survey and interviews were based on educated estimates and anecdotes. Nevertheless, clear patterns and trends have emerged that provide what may be the most comprehensive picture of the current state of undergraduate education at research universities. In the remainder of this chapter, I will examine some of these trends. In the concluding section, I will focus on administrative efforts at promoting institutional change.

Patterns and Trends

The Boyer Commission report was driven by the conviction that research universities are uniquely positioned to offer an undergraduate education that takes advantage of the immense resources of their research and graduate programs and that makes "research-based learning the standard" (Boyer Commission, 1998, p. 15). Providing such an education, the commission argued, required re-conceiving both the curriculum and prevailing modes of teaching and learning to bring inquiry-based learning to the fore and prepare students to participate in the intellectual life of the university. The survey and follow-up interviews suggest that three recommendations have attracted the most attention: engage undergraduates in research or a creative endeavor and make it the centerpiece of their education; construct a first-year experience that encourages active learning and critical skills development; and build on the first-year experience through a course of study epitomized by inquiry-based learning, collaborative experiences, and the development of written and oral communication skills that are at least at a standard reflective of a college degree.

Undergraduate Research and Creative Activity. More than anything else, the recommendation that a supervised research or creative undertaking be incorporated into the undergraduate experience resonated most strongly with faculty and administrators. The greatest activity has taken place in this arena. Whereas undergraduates at research universities had always been involved in research and scholarship, in recent years a substantial number of universities have begun to recognize that the opportunity to offer such experiences to undergraduates represents a real asset. Thus, they have devoted both attention and resources to expanding such opportunities and making them available to more students. Undergraduate research also has been emphasized in institutions' academic plans. Every university surveyed has mechanisms in place to support independent supervised work, and almost all are promoting and giving visibility to such activity. Departmental and campuswide events that showcase student projects are becoming increasingly common; more than half of all responding institutions regularly hold such events. Similarly, one-third of the institutions have Web-based or print journals (or both) in which students report on their work.

To further their research emphasis, institutions are increasingly centralizing their undergraduate research-related activities. Some 60 percent of research universities now have administrative offices that serve as a focal point for such activity. About 20 percent of these offices have authority and budget, set campuswide policies, and are generally responsible for promoting undergraduate research. More typically, undergraduate research offices have a service function that includes coordinating campus initiatives in this area, maintaining databases of opportunities for students on and off campus, helping students find appropriate research placements, and supporting or supplementing departmental efforts. Either way, departments remain central to the effort, and their commitment to undergraduate research and scholarship shapes the extent to which it is emphasized in the curriculum and in independent activity. Among universities that do not have centralized offices, about one-third have departmental structures. The remaining 7 percent do not have any organized structures. For this 40 percent of universities in which support for undergraduate research is decentralized, the roles and values of the department become even more important.

Campuses have been aggressive in seeking public and private funds to sustain and expand their undergraduate research emphasis; several universities have built requests for undergraduate research scholarships into their capital campaigns, and they have generally been successful. During the period 1998–2001, there appears to have been a substantial rise in funds available for this purpose.

Perhaps as a result of all this activity, the number and percentage of undergraduates participating in supervised research and scholarly activity by most reports have increased. In fact, many institutions cited increased student participation in research or creative activity as their most noteworthy achievement of the past few years. There has been a parallel rise in the number of faculty supervisors, with many of the new supervisors coming from professional schools and centers within the university, particularly in the health sciences, that do not have undergraduate programs. Interestingly, in the sciences, where most undergraduate research takes place, it is often difficult to engage faculty in innovative aspects of undergraduate education. Yet, faculty are enthusiastic about supervising students in their work, and they invest considerable time and resources in this activity.

Nevertheless, although the picture appears rosy, in what will emerge as a pattern in this discussion of elements within undergraduate education at research universities, serious challenges persist that are, or should be, of great concern to faculty and administrators. These challenges suggest that research and creative endeavors are still not central to the undergraduate mission at most institutions. A major challenge is how to involve more students. Despite the considerable progress that has been made in recent years, the number and percentage of undergraduates having a research experience remain relatively small and are often limited to the strongest students. Only seven institutions report having a research requirement for all graduates, five through independent, supervised projects and two through courses that have a substantial research component. Sixteen percent of research universities surveyed involve all or "most" (about 75 percent) of their undergraduates in these activities, 26 percent involve about half or all of their students in certain programs, and the remaining 48 percent of institutions involve some (about 25 percent) or "few" of their students. Nine percent of the surveyed universities could not provide estimates, reflecting the lack of quantitative information about undergraduate activity on some campuses. If research universities are going to be successful in their efforts to serve all students who want access to a research experience, campuses need to develop ways to create opportunities for a greater proportion of their large and diverse student population.

A second challenge relates to the unequal opportunities students have, depending on their major. The greatest student involvement in research occurs in laboratory sciences and engineering. Sixty-two percent of institutions responding to the Boyer survey reported that half or more of their laboratory science students engage in research; in engineering, 44 percent of institutions surveyed report that half or more of their students are involved in research. The two most active disciplines overall are biochemistry and psychology. The lowest student participation in independent activity is in nonlaboratory social sciences and humanities. In the social sciences, for example, only 25 percent of those responding to the Boyer survey reported participation by half or more of their students. Forty-nine percent reported lower participation, and the remainder could not answer the question, again pointing to the absence of meaningful data on many campuses. The picture in the humanities is even bleaker, as the percentage of institutions with half or more of their students engaged in scholarship dips to 21 percent, and 52 percent indicated lower participation. Twenty-seven percent of responding universities did not answer the question. Student participation in the creative and performing arts appears to fall midway, with 36 percent of all universities estimating that half or more of their students participate; 34 percent could not provide an estimate.

University officials recognize the need to extend opportunities to students in all disciplines and are concerned about those disciplines in which student participation is especially low. However, they are stymied by a lack of human and financial resources, a culture within some humanistic and social science departments that deters taking on undergraduates, few models to serve as good examples, and the lack of incentives to encourage faculty to take on students. Indeed, on some campuses in some disciplines, the push to involve students comes largely from outside the department. The question of how to engage humanities faculty and students has emerged as a major concern at regional network meetings of the Reinvention Center and promises to be a major agenda item for research universities.

A third issue relates to the large number of undergraduates that are taught at research universities. Although many agree with the goal of providing every student with a research experience, and three research universities among the survey respondents are successfully doing this, the vast majority of institutions surveyed indicated that they cannot, and some questioned whether engaging all students is even desirable. The main problems that survey respondents cite are a lack of resources and increasing pressures on faculty (particularly in the sciences), who are being asked to take on more and more students while maintaining active research programs. One selective private institution has gone so far as to impose an informal limit on the number of students per semester it can effectively accommodate.

Research universities face two challenges. One, as indicated, is involving significantly more students and, related to that, determining which students to target. The second is expanding the pool of qualified supervisors and identifying new venues and new resources to support their work. Increasingly, postdoctoral fellows, advanced graduate students, and highly trained technical staff are filling this role in the sciences and engineering. In the humanities and humanistic social sciences, there has been discussion recently about involving library faculty and technical staff, and a few universities have experimental programs in which graduate students are serving as supervisors. The search for new venues has led campuses to nearby hospitals, research laboratories, industrial research and development units, and community organizations.

When universities were asked in the survey to list the single most important thing their university could do to improve undergraduate education, not one mentioned undergraduate research and creative activity. This silence, taken together with their reported pride in their achievements in this area, suggests that they are generally satisfied that undergraduate research is a well-established enterprise on their campus and that their stated goals of increasing opportunities, involving more students, and giving visibility to students' research and creative achievements are being addressed. The follow-up interviews to the survey and the discussions at the Reinvention Center regional network meetings suggest, however, that much remains to be done. These conversations have made clear that the challenges identified here are real. Universities must respond to problems of identifying new resources and engaging all disciplines if undergraduate research and creative activity are going to become truly ingrained in the university culture and a central component of the education of a significant number of students.

First-Year Experience. The Boyer Commission's recommendation that research universities offer a first-year experience that will "provide new stimulation for intellectual growth and a firm grounding in inquiry-based learning and communication of information and ideas" (1998, p. 19) likewise has resonated with faculty and administrators, and here again, there has been considerable activity. More than 80 percent of the universities (seventy-six) that were part of the survey now offer some kind of academic seminar to first-year students. Within this group, about 40 percent enroll half or more of their freshman class in them. Only one institution reported having similar seminars for transfer students. At about half of the campuses, full-time regular faculty teach the seminars. At most other campuses, faculty often lead the seminars, assisted by staff, advanced graduate students, and at a few institutions, advanced undergraduate students. Five percent of institutions rely on adjuncts or part-time instructors. Three universities routinely invite emeriti faculty, who reportedly are among the most enthusiastic instructors—"the best faculty citizens." One campus is experimenting with an on-line seminar in which students interact with one another and a faculty instructor electronically.

As in the area of undergraduate research and creative activity, much progress has been seen on research university campuses as faculty and administrators have increasingly come to recognize the importance of the first-year experience and have taken concrete steps to offer an experience congruent with the Boyer Commission's goals. Again, however, most campuses are able to offer these courses to a relatively small proportion of their students. Although most would like to be able to accommodate more students—and a significant proportion have plans to do so—they are limited by the same lack of resources that impedes other undergraduate-focused efforts and by reluctance on the part of faculty to teach them. Institutions have been most successful in attracting faculty when they have provided incentives or have permitted faculty to decide the topic and develop the syllabus for the seminar. Some of the most innovative and successful seminars reportedly have involved two or more faculty as co-leaders. Several survey respondents observed that once faculty agree to offer a first-year seminar, they often "become hooked" and not only do it again but endeavor to recruit colleagues. Survey respondents also noted that one unanticipated benefit of teaching a freshman seminar is that it enhances faculty interest in pedagogy and becomes a powerful tool for training faculty to work with all students.

About 65 percent of research universities have responded to the call for an integrated first-year experience through block scheduling, in which the same cohort of students typically takes two or three courses together. This approach, advocates maintain, has the advantage of providing students with a supportive social environment and a superior academic experience. It is not surprising, therefore, that the greatest interest has been at the largest institutions, whereas experimentation with block scheduling at small institutions has been minimal.

The scope of block-scheduling initiatives varies enormously. Some represent an alternative path to fulfilling some general education requirements and thus attract a wide range of students. Others, such as engineering, have a disciplinary focus. A third group targets specific populations, such as commuters, underrepresented students in the sciences, or students at risk. About half of block-schedule programs include an integrative seminar typically taught by a faculty member.

Because of the constraints blocks impose on student schedules and course options and the enormous time they demand of faculty and staff, most campuses offer only a limited number of blocks units, and only a small proportion of their entering classes typically enroll. Half of the institutions that use block scheduling reported enrolling fewer than 25 percent of their incoming students. In the follow-up interviews, six campuses indicated enrolling fewer than 5 percent. Only one large public research university is endeavoring to enroll all its incoming students in blocks.

Block scheduling may well represent an experiment that works well in only limited situations. Block programs are costly to run because they require considerable support staff to coordinate activities, and they typically have a high attrition rate (in the blocks) after the first semester. The one institution, however, that is extending block scheduling to all students has found that it increases overall retention. Students who drop out reportedly do so because they feel confined in their academic choices, complain that the rigid scheduling prevents them from pursuing simultaneously sched-uled interests, and perceive the blocks as limiting their opportunities to meet other students. Few institutions plan to expand block scheduling, maintaining that its primary value is in recruiting students ("Parents like them") and in helping them adjust to the university.

Another similar approach to an integrated first-year experience has been through the establishment of learning communities, which are often organized around specific themes and made up of students with shared interests. Many of these communities are residential. Although the Boyer survey did not include specific questions about learning communities or the extent to which this model has been adopted, several respondents volun-teered that their administrations are increasingly forming or considering forming such communities. The goals appear to be social as well as academic and reflect a common interest in creating a friendlier and more welcoming environment for incoming students. This interest was well expressed in the Boyer Commission report: "Research universities should foster a community of learners. Large research universities must find ways . . . to help students develop small communities within the larger whole" (1998, p. 34). Although a movement toward learning communities appears likely, respondents noted that it will be a challenge to engage fac-ulty and others in the communities. A second challenge, based on the block-scheduling experience, will be to ensure that the communities are seen by students as both enriching and flexible—as desirable rather than restrictive alternatives.

Building on the First-Year Experience. The Boyer Commission envi-sioned the first year as introducing students to "the wealth, diversity, scale, and scope of what lies ahead" (1998, p. 19) in their education at a research university, instilling excitement at the sense of discovery that permeates the environment, and providing a foundation that would enable them to move forward. Their remaining years at the university were to be used to build on this foundation to develop and refine their intellectual capabilities. Such growth would be facilitated by an undergraduate education that encompasses an integrative, interdisciplinary curriculum; collaborative and inquiry-based teaching and learning; written and oral communication infused throughout their course of study; and a capstone experience that would enable students to pull together their various strands of learning and develop them further through a senior thesis or other major project.

Few of these aspects of undergraduate education have attracted as much attention at research universities as the emphases on independent research and creative endeavor and the first-year experience. This is largely because much of students' subsequent education is within their major, and responsibility for it lies within departments and schools. Few campuses surveyed or participating in follow-up interviews or Reinvention Center network meetings have mechanisms to foster an overall comprehensive consideration of upper-class programs. Following the first year, the one additional area that has attracted university-wide attention has been general education, which cuts across several departments and units. Within general education, there has been considerable effort and creativity in breaking down disciplinary barriers and transmitting knowledge in new forms. One method is through team-taught courses in which students examine broadly defined subjects from the perspectives of several disciplines. Another new, growing, and more radical approach is to re-conceive general education so that instead of being content based, it consists of a range of cognitive and technical literacies that students must demonstrate to graduate. Breaking with the traditional menu-driven general education in which students take a specified number of courses in designated categories, this new model allows students to achieve literacy through noncurricular as well as curricular venues. The goal is to enable them to incorporate the full range of experiences that comprise their undergraduate education, such as travel abroad (to satisfy a language literacy requirement) or directing a project to construct a robot (to satisfy a technical literacy requirement) and afford them a flexibility that more conventional models do not have. Virtually every campus surveyed or interviewed seems to have instituted some kind of change in its general education in recent years.

Written and Oral Communication Skills. The highest priority in general education has been to facilitate the development of good writing skills. In recent years, almost all of the institutions that were part of the survey have increased their writing requirements, and a substantial number want to do even more. More than half (52 percent) have a two-semester writing requirement; a smaller percentage (43 percent) requires one semester. Beyond these requirements, 38 percent of responding universities offer additional lower-division writing courses, 51 percent offers upper-division writing courses, and 32 percent has incorporated extensive writing into the major. Increasingly, institutions are employing trained staff to assist faculty to develop and teach the writing component of their courses. Ten percent of survey respondents identified the development or enhancement of their writing programs as being among their major improvements in recent years; a similar percentage listed improving the teaching of writing on their agenda for the next three years.

Whereas faculty and administrators are concerned about students' lack of oral communication skills, few institutions have implemented campuswide requirements to facilitate skills in speaking. Only 19 percent of survey respondents reported that oral communications skills are taught in their university's introductory courses. Several institutions offer a communication major. In addition to the major, oral communication courses are mostly required in professionally oriented undergraduate majors, such as engineering, management, education, and agriculture. The main venues for students to develop oral communication skills are campus forums where students give presentations on their research. Such opportunities, however, are available to only a limited number of students. Despite the lack of formal attention given to oral communication, several respondents noted that electives in subjects such as rhetoric and public speaking are becoming increasingly popular.

Inquiry-Based Learning. Based on the survey and interviews, faculty and administrators are clearly thinking and talking about inquiry-based learning and apparently incorporating it in their teaching. Furthermore, universities are spending considerable amounts of money establishing centers to train faculty in inquiry-based and other pedagogies. About 65 percent of all survey respondents reported that their university encourages inquiry-based teaching and has mechanisms to help faculty develop skills in using this method. Most (73 percent) of those with such mechanisms reported some degree of curricular or pedagogical change in recent years as a result. At the same time, there is no consensus as to either what the term "inquiry-based learning" means or how or to what extent it is being applied in instructional settings. One survey respondent summarizes the situation well: "Inquiry-based learning has been a buzzword for several years. Many courses/instructors say it is a characteristic of what they do, but no one has agreed on what exactly it is." Similarly, another respondent notes: "Our sense is that inquiry-based approaches are forming an increasing part of a number of introductory courses, but we have no data and have not gathered systematic information."

Among respondents able to provide data on inquiry-based teaching and learning in introductory courses, about 25 percent reported its use in many introductory courses, 25 percent in "several key" courses, and 50 percent in a few courses. The greatest emphasis appears to be in core introductory courses, especially in calculus and chemistry

Collaborative Learning and Teaching. In contrast with other aspects of undergraduate education, little university-wide attention has been given to promoting collaborative learning or teaching, and it apparently has not taken hold. Only a small proportion (about 15 percent) of research universities that

were part of the survey consider collaborative learning an important curriculum issue. The extent to which it is occurring on an individual campus
varies by school within the university, by department, by course, and by
individual course instructors. About 43 percent of the surveyed institutions
report that it is promoted in some departments or programs, and 34 percent
say it is a topic of discussion. About 50 percent of all the survey respondents
reported collaborative learning in some other introductory courses, and
about 60 percent reported collaborative learning in some courses in majors.
Fewer than 10 percent reported collaborative learning in many introductory
courses or many courses in majors. Team approaches to teaching and learning appear to be most prevalent in engineering and management, where they
are deemed highly successful. Officials who were interviewed as a follow-up
to the survey suggested that faculty who employed cooperative activities in
their classrooms were generally pleased with the outcomes, and they anticipated a slow but gradual rise in such activities.

Efforts at collaborative teaching have been equally sporadic and
dependent largely on faculty and departmental initiatives. In fact, the one
area in which team teaching has made inroads is in general education,
which cuts across departments and units. The apparent disinterest among
faculty in science disciplines in experimenting with collaborative models
of teaching is somewhat ironic because science faculty often collaborate in
their research. Some respondents noted "structural impediments" to collaborative teaching. Among those cited were procedures that discourage
team-teaching courses and methods for linking resource allocation to
departments with student enrollments in the courses they offer.

Capstone Courses and Senior Projects. The Boyer Commission conceived of the undergraduate experience as culminating in a capstone project that "marshaled" all the research skills students developed earlier in
their studies and that demanded "the framing of a significant question or
set of questions, the research or creative exploration to find answers, and
the communication skills to convey the results to an audience"(1998, p.
27). Although survey and interview participants themselves recognized the
value of such an experience, few of their universities have instituted a capstone requirement for all of their students or undertaken a campuswide discussion on the merit of doing so. The most common pattern is a scattered
one in which some individual majors or programs require a capstone
course, senior seminar, or senior thesis. Across all universities, major senior projects are required almost uniformly by honors programs, for departmental and university honors degrees, and in engineering departments.
Seventy-one percent of the survey respondents reported capstone requirements in some majors or programs, 5 percent said that they were required
of all undergraduates, and 12 percent indicated that they were completely
optional.

The decision to institute a capstone requirement resides with departments; this gives rise to the variability that exists on most campuses. That

honors programs that consistently have such a requirement are university-wide programs is probably no coincidence. As with collaborative learning, it may be that establishing a capstone requirement for all students will require a university-wide initiative that transcends the departmental level.

Institutional Efforts

There is no question that research universities—whether public or private, large or small, comprehensive or specialized—are giving increased attention to undergraduate education. At virtually every institution surveyed, administrative leaders and faculty are talking and thinking about the way undergraduate education is conceived and transmitted to an extent they had not previously. The impulse to raise the status of undergraduate teaching and learning has come from the top. Presidents and provosts now routinely offer their own and their institution's vision of undergraduate education in major addresses and reports to the public and to their university communities, and they make clear that it is a key element on their agendas. In so doing, they frequently cite the Boyer Commission report and link their efforts directly to commission recommendations. Perhaps in response to the recognition that this emphasis resonates well with the public, they also are increasingly incorporating components of undergraduate education into their university's fundraising efforts and into their marketing and recruiting materials.

Administrative leaders, moreover, have often followed up on this newly articulated interest with highly visible actions. The most common of these appears to be the establishment of teaching resource centers whose mission is to assist faculty to improve their teaching, whether by helping them to rethink their goals for their students, to redesign course syllabi, or to try new pedagogical approaches. Almost every research university surveyed now has such a center; about 10 percent of the Boyer survey respondents listed its establishment among the most important developments on their campus in the three years immediately following publication of the Boyer Commission report. For a significant number of respondents, the challenge is to persuade their faculty to view the center as a valuable resource and to get them to take advantage of its services. Faculty, many noted, have difficulty seeing the connections between their teaching and student learning or imagining the benefits they themselves would derive, and they have been reluctant to seek assistance from center staff. The most successful centers are either or both those that are proactive in approaching faculty and departments and those that focus their efforts on specific disciplines or on areas where they have special expertise, such as in the creative use of technology in different instructional settings. A few campuses have offered incentives to encourage faculty participation. One university, for example, has experimented with giving laptop computers to every faculty member who attends a workshop on instructional technology.

Another highly visible approach adopted by university leaders has been to convene campuswide task forces to examine aspects of undergraduate education and to organize forums designed to energize and engage faculty. About one-fourth of the respondents to the Boyer Commission survey referred to these kinds of developments.

A third action has been to establish a new position (or strengthen an existing one) of vice president, provost, or dean for undergraduate education. This position is intended to give focus, provide leadership, and serve as an advocate for undergraduate studies. Equally important, it signifies the institution's support and commitment to its undergraduate enterprise. A significant portion of the institutions surveyed now have this position in place, although the titles, roles, responsibilities, and budgets of the incumbents vary enormously by campus, as do the extent to which the incumbents exert influence or "have a seat at the table" equivalent to their counterparts in graduate studies. A few campuses have integrated responsibility for undergraduate and graduate education into one position to emphasize their essential connectedness and the equal value they place on both.

When these administrative positions in undergraduate education were created, their importance, as several respondents observed, was as much symbolic as real. Yet, as one incumbent noted, "the symbolism has great value because it suggests authority." Indeed, to varying degrees, individuals in this position appear to be developing a constituency among the faculty and taking the lead in encouraging experimentation; promoting curricular innovation, particularly in general education, to address the kinds of deficiencies identified by the Boyer Commission; and instituting new programs and initiatives, including some directed at faculty. In fact, as the survey revealed, the areas in which the greatest activity has occurred have been those that have been initiated and supported by the university's leadership, usually through this new position.

Almost all campuses surveyed have undertaken widely publicized efforts to emphasize and reward good teaching. Most institutions offer grants and other incentives to faculty to encourage curricular and pedagogical innovation and faculty participation in professional development activities. *All* responding institutions have mechanisms to recognize excellence in teaching. They range from distinguished teaching awards to salary supplements for teaching key courses to merit raises, to released time for curriculum development. Further, these recognitions may be bestowed at every level (that is, departmental, divisional, college, university, or system). Often these awards are presented at highly public ceremonies. Moreover, whereas "teaching excellence" historically referred exclusively to the quality of classroom instruction, in recent years, there has been a growing recognition of the many contributions faculty can make. About half of the survey respondents reported that their campus has expanded its definition of teaching excellence to encompass the full range of activities that enrich the undergraduate experience, such as supervision of independent work, curricular innovation, serving on key committees, providing leadership in undergraduate education within a department, or obtaining external funding for an educational initiative.

Finally, administrative leaders have actively promoted changes in promotion-and-tenure policies to reflect the greater value the institution is placing on undergraduate teaching. Almost half of those responding to the survey reported instituting such changes in recent years. At 35 percent of the universities, officials described undergraduate teaching as a "major" consideration in promotion-and-tenure decisions. At other campuses, it was viewed as a "limited" consideration or one that varied by department. To reinforce the new weight they are placing on undergraduate teaching, some campuses are experimenting with teaching portfolios and other tools that summarize faculty teaching activities and provide student evaluations.

A major challenge for university leaders is to convince their faculty that the revised promotion-and-tenure guidelines represent genuine priorities on campus and will be implemented. Almost every administrator who participated in the survey indicated that candidates would be denied tenure even if they were productive researchers if their research productivity is not accompanied by attention to teaching. At the same time, faculty who were interviewed in conjunction with the survey or who took part in Reinvention Center network discussions uniformly agreed that, regardless of what the new guidelines state, in promotion-and-tenure deliberations, the emphasis will remain on research productivity, and little consideration will be given to undergraduate teaching.

The Big Picture

As the survey and follow-up discussions have found, research universities have made considerable headway in the past five years in bringing undergraduate education to the fore and transforming many of its core elements. Whereas in this chapter I have focused on broad academic and administrative issues, similar rethinking and experimentation have occurred in the curricular, pedagogical, and social arenas, and the new interest in undergraduate education has even led to a redesign of some physical facilities. The Boyer Commission report clearly has been instrumental in promoting the recent activity. A substantial number of institutions queried indicated that they used the report as "ammunition" to focus attention on their campus on undergraduate education and to facilitate discussion. In several instances, institutions cited the report in grant applications, accreditation studies, fundraising activities, and efforts to gain targeted resources from state legislatures and boards of trustees.

"Headway" and institutional transformation, however, are not the same thing, and the ultimate goal of the Boyer Commission and others who have been troubled about the state of undergraduate education at research universities has been to stimulate genuine transformation. The experience of the past five years provides a basis for optimism, although with some caveats. Above all, it suggests that supportive leadership, structures, and resources are all necessary to bring about substantive change. Faculty and departmental willingness to participate is equally important.

When university leaders stepped forward and demonstrated by word and act their interest in raising the status and improving the quality of the undergraduate education their institutions offered, they were joined by a surprising number of colleagues who shared this interest. Some of their major actions have been highly focused and visible and in areas most amenable to change. Although initially perceived by many as largely symbolic, they have produced some of the most exciting and important innovations that have taken place, and they have engaged a large and diverse group of faculty. It is this group that has spearheaded many of the successful initiatives discussed here, specifically, the considerable rise in undergraduate research activity, the development and implementation of integrative first-year experiences, the enhancement of writing requirements, and the significant revisions of general education. The progress has been less noteworthy in areas of undergraduate education in which responsibilities lie with departments.

A persistent problem is that the best educational developments often reach only a small proportion of an institution's undergraduates, frequently the most academically talented ones and ones in special programs. Unless ways are found to scale up these efforts to benefit a wider spectrum, and unless more faculty step forward to participate, they will have only a marginal effect and reinforce the notion that the leadership is not serious and that most of the activity has indeed been symbolic.

Thus, strong leadership must be accompanied by a fundamental acceptance by faculty and departments of the centrality of undergraduate education in the mission of research universities if transformation is to occur. They need to see connections between their roles as scholars and as teachers. A curious paradox, or perhaps tension, exists. Faculty participating in the survey interviews and Reinvention Center network meetings almost uniformly agreed that change requires faculty and departmental support because the real locus of power at research universities resides with departments. Departments set the agenda, develop and implement the undergraduate curriculum and requirements, assign instructors, and supervise students in independent work. Faculty, departments, and deans, however, have in many instances been slow in taking up the new challenges, as evidenced in their varied responses to such practices as collaborative teaching and instituting capstone courses. They point to the realities of the research universities' continuing emphases on research productivity, national rankings of their graduate departments, their already-expanding responsibilities, and their own interest in pursing research and scholarship. Some say they sought work at a research university precisely because of its focus on research and graduate training. Others express concern that if they devote too much time and energy to teaching, they will be marginalized within their own departments and lose mobility. These are familiar refrains, yet they cannot be dismissed. Reinvention is not likely to occur unless there is re-prioritizing within departments and disciplines, yet little attention has been directed at them. Furthermore, the national and professional associations with which faculty identify must be brought into the discussion, to rethink their own values and priorities to encourage and support an undergraduate education in which research and scholarly activity are key components.

Collectively, the patterns and trends reported in this chapter demonstrate the extent to which the Boyer Commission and others' calls for transformation have been taken seriously by research university leaders and have begun to infuse both the vision and daily operations of these institutions. Undergraduate education is now more central to their mission than it was previously, and there appears to be a subtle shift in attitudes and values among a growing number of faculty and administrators. Thus, the foundation for fundamental institutional change exists. It is, however, a thin foundation affecting the teaching and learning of a relatively small proportion of undergraduates and faculty.

The next challenge for universities is to expand, integrate, and sustain the successful practices and programs they have implemented in recent years so that they are available to students at different levels and benefit most of the students. There remain, however, serious structural and financial impediments. Most research universities are now operating under severe budgetary restraints.

The kind of undergraduate education promulgated in the Boyer Commission report, as well as in other reports, is labor intensive and expensive. One response has been an increasing reliance on non-tenure track instruction, especially in such critical areas as writing, language, and basic laboratory instruction. More and more this instructional role is being filled by adjuncts, postdoctoral fellows, graduate students, and fixed-term instructors. This group collectively is rarely addressed in discussions of undergraduate education. Survey respondents expressed concern over this and also called for hiring more full-time faculty, particularly in departments that are most affected by growing enrollments and revised general education. Public research universities must work closely with state legislatures to make sure that adequate resources follow the mandates to increase enrollment.

In a final analysis, institutional transformation cannot be achieved by the institution itself. Research university leaders can define and communicate their vision of undergraduate education and take major steps on their campuses to achieve it—as most have. Sustaining their considerable efforts, overcoming impediments, and moving forward will require a combination of efforts on the parts not only of faculty and administrators but also of national and professional organizations and both public and private university governing boards.

References

American Council on Education. *Educating One-Third of a Nation: The Conference Report.* Washington, D.C.: American Council on Education, 1988.

Bok, D. *Universities, and the Future of America.* Durham, N.C.: Duke University Press, 1990.

Boyer Commission on Educating Undergraduates in the Research University, S. S. Kenny (chair). *Reinventing Undergraduate Education: A Blueprint for America's Research Universities.* State University of New York–Stony Brook, 1998.

Boyer Commission on Educating Undergraduates in the Research University, S. S. Kenny (chair). *Reinventing Undergraduate Education: Three Years After the Boyer Report.* State University of New York–Stony Brook, 2002.

Boyer, E. L. *College: The Undergraduate Experience in America.* New York: Harper & Row, 1987.

Boyer, E. L. *Scholarship Reconsidered: Priorities of the Professoriate.* Carnegie Foundation for the Advancement of Teaching. Princeton, N.J.: Princeton University Press, 1990.

Cheney, L. *50 Hours: A Core Curriculum for College Students.* Washington, D.C.: National Endowment for the Humanities, 1989.

Matyas, M. L., and Malcolm, S. M. (eds.). *Investing in Human Potential: Science and Engineering at the Crossroads.* Washington, D.C.: American Association for the Advancement of Science, 1991.

National Commission on Excellence in Education. *A Nation at Risk.* Washington, D.C.: U.S. Department of Education, 1983.

National Science Board, Task Committee on Undergraduate Science and Engineering Education, H. A. Neal (Chair). *Undergraduate Science, Mathematics and Engineering Education; Role for the National Science Foundation and Recommendations for Action by Other Sectors to Strengthen Collegiate Education and Pursue Excellence in the Next Generation of U.S. Leadership in Science and Technology.* National Science Foundation publication no. NSB 86–100. Washington, D.C.: National Science Foundation, 1986.

National Science Foundation. *Gaining the Competitive Edge: Critical Issues in Science and Engineering Technician Education.* T. Collins, D. Gentry, and V. Crawley (co-chairs). Workshop on Critical Issues in Science and Engineering Technician Education. National Science Foundation publication no. NSF 94–32. Washington, D.C.: National Science Foundation, 1993.

Seymour, E., and Hewitt, N. *Talking About Leaving: Factors Contributing to High Attrition Rates Among Science, Mathematics, and Engineering Undergraduate Majors.* Boulder: Bureau of Sociological Research, University of Colorado, 1994.

Sigma Xi. *An Exploration of the Nature and Quality of Undergraduate Education in Science, Mathematics, and Engineering.* A Report of the National Advisory Group of Sigma XI, The Scientific Research Society, sponsored by the National Science Foundation and the Johnson Foundation, The Wingspread Meeting, Racine, Wisc., Jan. 23–26, 1989. [http://www.sigmaxi.org/resources/publications/descriptions.shtml]. Access date: Jan. 23, 2003.

Wilson, R. "Report Blasts Research Universities for Poor Teaching of Undergraduates." *Chronicle of Higher Education,* 44(33), A12-A13, Apr. 24, 1998.

WENDY KATKIN *is the director of the Reinvention Center at Stony Brook, New York, a national center established in 2000 to provide leadership in promoting an undergraduate education at research universities that builds on their unique resources and is synergistic with their research and graduate training activities.*

3

Snapshots of undergraduate research programs at research universities offer models and ideas as benchmark programs.

Undergraduate Research at the Research Universities

Carolyn Ash Merkel

American research universities offer students a diverse, rich, and dynamic environment that promotes academic rigor and intellectual and personal growth. They provide students the unique opportunities to learn in the research environment and to explore the intellectual universe with faculty who are engaged in the creation of knowledge at the frontiers of their disciplines. Students can sample widely from abundant academic offerings and become intellectually nimble and well prepared to continue their education or launch their careers.

However, the universities in general have been criticized loudly for their emphasis on research over teaching and for not committing enough of their vast resources to the education of undergraduates. Institutions have been challenged to involve students in the research enterprise and to offer more of them hands-on experiences to enhance their learning.

At least a few undergraduates have always been involved in research; they have been the students who distinguish themselves to their professors. And in some universities, it is still the top students who get to do research. The quiet students, or those who have not achieved high grade-point averages, are not invited to participate in research. That situation began to change with the creation of successful undergraduate research programs at some universities and with the founding of organizations that support the enterprise.

Over time, some universities have increased institutional emphasis on learning by doing. The Massachusetts Institute of Technology (MIT) developed its Undergraduate Research Opportunities Program in 1969 to allow any student to start doing research. Ten years later, the California Institute of Technology (Caltech) initiated its Summer Undergraduate Research Fellowships program to offer summer research opportunities to students. The Council on Undergraduate Research (CUR) was founded in 1978. By the mid-1980s, the National Science Foundation (NSF) created its Research Experiences for Undergraduates program. The National Conferences on Undergraduate Research held its first event in 1987.

In 1987, the Carnegie Foundation published *College: The Undergraduate Experience in America*, which concluded that undergraduates at large research universities were less satisfied with their college experiences than peers at other kinds of institutions (Grassmuck, 1990). In *Scholarship Reconsidered* (1990), Boyer challenged universities to "break out of the tired old teaching versus research debate and define in more creative ways what it means to be a scholar" (p. xii). He went on to propose that universities strengthen research, integration, application, and teaching, starting at the highest levels of university administration (p. xii). State legislatures took up the call and pressured their public universities to reform undergraduate education ("Transforming the State Role in Undergraduate Education," 1986, p. 13).

All these efforts taken together began the difficult and slow process of changing the landscape of undergraduate education. However, the 1998 report of the Boyer Commission on Educating Undergraduates in the Research University, *Reinventing Undergraduate Education: A Blueprint for America's Research Universities*, indicted the universities for their lack of progress in the realm of reinvigorating undergraduate education. That report further stimulated activity in the research universities.

In this chapter, I describe the undergraduate research culture and draw a picture of undergraduate research at four research universities, including Caltech, MIT, Rutgers, and the University of Washington, all of which exemplify strong undergraduate research cultures. The information was gathered in a study done for the Association of American Universities in 2000. The purpose of the project was to characterize undergraduate research at these institutions to identify issues, questions, opportunities, and barriers affecting undergraduate research in the sciences and engineering and in the arts and humanities. I interviewed close to two hundred administrators, faculty members, and students, and the snapshots of undergraduate research have been developed from these conversations.

Nature of Undergraduate Research at the Research Universities

Undergraduate research in the research universities has particular features. It is first and foremost an educational opportunity for the student. The focus of undergraduate research is on the academic growth of the students rather than on the development of the faculty member, although many junior faculty members launch their research programs with the help of undergraduates.

These faculty are often eager to work with students because their own undergraduate research experiences set them on their professional courses. Students in the research universities work with mentors at the forefront of their fields. They often have access to state-of-the-art research equipment, materials, and supplies and other resources the institution can offer.

Undergraduate research helps to address the issue raised by the media and the public that research universities emphasize research over teaching to the detriment of the students. Most academics view research and teaching as a continuum, with each activity influencing and informing the other, rather than as two separate or opposite activities. Although the faculty reward system is driven by research productivity and (secondarily) by teaching, faculty generally view undergraduate research as part of their teaching responsibilities. For most students, hands-on experiences provide the best learning tools. The essence of undergraduate research is the supportive, encouraging, intellectual partnership between students and other researchers and through which students apply knowledge gained in the classroom to new questions and problems.

Undergraduate research promotes students' inclusion in the community of scholars described by Boyer in *Scholarship Reconsidered* (1990). As they become collaborators with their mentors or colleagues within a research group, students become junior partners in the research enterprise. Faculty mentors provide overall guidance and coaching. They help students sink their roots in the culture of the discipline. Mentors provide advice on graduate school or career development. They also write the all-important letters of recommendation for graduate or professional school or for jobs in industry. Often the relationships formed through undergraduate research last many years, and mentors and protégés continue their interaction as the student moves through his or her education and into a career. For most students, engaging in undergraduate research is an introduction to research. However, many students make significant contributions to the mentor's ongoing work, often becoming coauthors of articles in the refereed literature.

The progress from one level of education to the next becomes more seamless and efficient through undergraduate research. Undergraduates participate with graduate students and postdoctoral fellows in the stimulation and challenges of doing research. Students learn firsthand what it is like to be a graduate student before they make the commitment to years of additional study and research. Graduate students and postdoctoral fellows develop mentoring skills they will need as they move into their own careers. Undergraduate research provides a junction in the educational continuum.

Students often choose to attend research universities because of the opportunities to learn in an environment heavily influenced by the ongoing creation of new knowledge and for the options to get involved in research. Universities may include an undergraduate fellowship as part of the recruitment package. Some students strive to find research opportunities in which they can be involved. Others, perhaps most, must be invited into the research experience. They must be encouraged and shown that they, too, can learn the skills, techniques, and methods; do research; gain the benefits of original exploration; and participate in the scholarly community.

Culture

Many universities have developed a culture of undergraduate research. In some institutions, this environment has evolved because of specific characteristics of the university. The focus on the undergraduate experience promotes the concept of students working with faculty members. Other schools have taken deliberate steps to create a supportive climate and to encourage undergraduate research for many (or most) students. For the purposes of this discussion, it will be useful to consider the elements of a culture of undergraduate research within an institution.

In an institution with a pervasive undergraduate research culture, the major campus constituencies—administration, faculty, and students—participate in and are integral to the enterprise. The administration is proactive in enhancing undergraduate education in general and encouraging undergraduate research in particular. The administration has included undergraduate research in the central mission or strategic plan and has articulated an overarching vision for the role of undergraduate research in the academic experience of its students. It has allocated human and financial resources to the enterprise. The benefits accruing to students, faculty, and the institution are well known and widely publicized. The administration has helped to form an institutional expectation of mentoring undergraduate students as part of the teaching mission of the university.

When faculty discuss undergraduate research, they display evidence of institutional conversation about the enterprise. They talk about the importance and value of undergraduate research and scholarly or creative activities in the larger context of the university curriculum, pedagogy, and broad educational opportunities. Faculty are committed to the development of undergraduates and think creatively about how to bring students into the scholarly community. Many faculty mentor students, either in one-to-one or one-to-many relationships. Faculty use a common language to talk about how they involve students in research, and there is a general understanding of what the term "undergraduate research" means within the institution as a whole and in the colleges and departments.

Students at these universities know that the institution encourages their participation in research and scholarly activities, and they are well aware of available opportunities to get involved. They know what programs are in place, and they know how to get involved. Students take the initiative to educate themselves and their peers about research. They may form "undergraduate research clubs"—a community of undergraduate scholars—and may invite faculty or visitors to give seminars, develop an undergraduate research journal (either on-line or hard copy) to showcase their work, or create Web sites to advertise opportunities to peers and recruit faculty mentors. These groups also give students a forum to exchange knowledge and ideas flowing from their own research projects.

A culture of undergraduate research strengthens universities, and institutions reap rewards as they invest in their students. The competition for excellent students is intense, and institutions aim to recruit the best students possible. As well-informed consumers of education, students seek, and expect, outstanding opportunities. Curious, motivated students complement excellent faculty. Students who take advantage of these opportunities are more satisfied with their undergraduate experiences and are more apt to become happy alumni who want to "give back" to their university through financial gifts or personal involvement. The large public universities are under pressure from the media, state legislatures, and other agencies to improve the undergraduate experience. Undergraduate research programs address many of these criticisms and provide good examples of successful educational programs.

Differences Between Private and Public Institutions

Significant differences exist among the 135 research universities in the United States, and each institution has a unique environment even as all universities share common characteristics. Public institutions face significant challenges and issues in developing a culture of undergraduate research that the smaller private universities do not have. The public institutions are large, complex organizations subdivided into colleges and further into departments and programs, and undergraduate research may flourish in some areas but not in others. The administration may not always know what programs exist in the departments. These institutions must respond to and are accountable to state legislatures and other public agencies, another layer of oversight with tremendous influence on university policies.

Extremely diverse undergraduate student bodies with widely varying degrees of ability, preparation, and interest inhabit the public institutions. Many students hold part-time or even full-time jobs, and academic pursuits become a sideline occupation. Many students choose research universities because they want to learn in the environment where new knowledge is created and forefront work is carried out, and others have not considered the research environment at all. The assertive students put themselves forward to meet potential mentors and express their desire to get involved in research. The quiet students can get through these schools knowing few administrators and fewer faculty and without participating in research. Student-faculty partnerships also improve student retention (Nagda and others, 1998).

Faculty have teaching responsibility for large classes and get to know only the students who stand out. They may invite those students who have excellent academic records or who they identify as bright and curious to join their research endeavors. The quiet students can blend into the masses and be overlooked, although they may possess skills and abilities equal to other students.

An administration faces challenges as it seeks to institutionalize undergraduate research. Providing one-to-one mentoring of students is impossible, so the university has to discover one-to-many options to give students hands-on experiences. The public universities possess resources that can support and expand undergraduate research. For example, faculty in professional schools can increase the mentor pool for undergraduates seeking research opportunities. Available resources have to be identified and perhaps reallocated. That makes everyone nervous!

The private institutions have different challenges, advantages, and resources. They are smaller, so the school can be more selective in admitting students. The ratio of students to faculty is lower. Members of the administration and faculty can get to know students individually. The private schools can offer many, perhaps most, students one-to-one mentoring opportunities. They are generally not bound by governmental policies, which dictate certain activities in the public universities. They may be administratively leaner than the public universities and, therefore, more nimble as they set about developing an undergraduate research culture. The competition for excellent students can be a primary driver in revitalizing undergraduate education. Students are increasingly educated consumers as they apply to universities, and many seek institutions that offer a strong curriculum and broad opportunities.

Undergraduate Research at Four Universities

This section provides more depth on programs at Rutgers, the University of Washington, MIT, and Caltech.

Rutgers University. Rutgers, the state university of New Jersey, has been remarkably successful in cultivating a culture of undergraduate research. The main campus at New Brunswick has an undergraduate student body of twenty-eight thousand students, and about seven thousand graduate students matriculated into ten colleges. Since 1970, under strong leadership by the administration, Rutgers has grown from a well-regarded undergraduate institution into a research university.

About 1990, the university's new president, Francis G. Lawrence, developed initiatives—including undergraduate research—to enhance the academic life of its students. The administration included these initiatives in the university's strategic plan, and Rutgers has taken bold steps to develop a culture that values undergraduate education and promotes undergraduate research. The results of the efforts may be seen in many administrative actions.

The president created the office of the Vice President for Undergraduate Education, and the vice president, Susan G. Forman, has been innovative in enhancing the curriculum, including the development of an undergraduate research program. In identifying ongoing undergraduate research opportunities and reviewing the barriers to student involvement, she recognized that students were ignorant of the available opportunities. They often saw research and teaching as opposites; they did not see themselves as members of the community of scholars, able to participate in the creation of new knowledge. She took a simple but important step in distributing to every sophomore a brochure describing undergraduate research and how to participate. She recruited academic advisors to encourage students to start doing research. She built upon activities already in place. For example, to showcase ongoing undergraduate research activities that have been housed in the various colleges, she created "research weeks" each spring to publicize over sixty undergraduate research events in all departments. Students and faculty like the smaller departmental or college programs, but the small events are publicized as part of a larger activity. It attracts attention university-wide and beyond the campus to the community.

Forman created the University-wide Fellows Program as a centerpiece of the effort to emphasize undergraduate research. Through the program, faculty members apply for funding to support the student. The funds may be used for a student stipend, or the mentor might take the student to a conference or use the money to purchase special materials the student will require in the research. Articles about the fellows and mentors appear in campus publications to disseminate information about the program and bring focus to the undergraduate research enterprise.

Undergraduate research is prominently featured on the Rutgers Web site within one click of the front page. Directly linked to the front page is the following description: "Curiosity about the world and a commitment to solving problems—these are the passions that drive a research university. At Rutgers, a member of the prestigious Association of American Universities, both graduate and undergraduate students work side-by-side with renowned professors, studying such intriguing topics as the nature of dark matter in the universe, bioinformatics, and the genetic basis for diseases" (http://www.rutgers.edu/research.shtml).

The university created a Teaching Excellence Center with institutional funds to provide training for faculty in new instructional technology, help them overcome the "sage-on-the-stage" approach to lecturing, and assist them in developing a variety of active learning methods for use in their classrooms, including inquiry-based courses. An example of the move to inquiry-based courses may be seen in the genetics course that serves 1,000 students. Beginning in fall 2000, all students are assigned a gene to investigate. With funds from an NSF Institution-wide Reform Grant, new science courses for nonscience majors were created to provide inquiry-based learning. As one administrator said about these changes, "It will be different from lectures. It brings Rutgers closer to the new curriculum that will be commonplace in ten years."

Faculty and administrators at Rutgers accept a broad definition of the term *undergraduate research*. Although aspects of the definition vary from discipline to discipline, faculty largely agree that students who participate substantively in the work of the faculty member are doing undergraduate research. The university has expressed its commitment to expanding opportunities, and raising funds to support it will be one of the requests in an upcoming capital campaign.

Rutgers has been successful in the steps it has taken so far to enhance undergraduate research opportunities for its students. The Commission on Higher Education of the Middle States Association of Schools and Colleges reaccredited Rutgers in 1998. The self-study featured undergraduate education, including research and creative activity, as one of four topic areas. The accreditation report stated, "Two aspects of undergraduate education are particularly deserving of commendation: (1) the emphasis on providing undergraduate student research opportunities and (2) in a more general way, the attentiveness of faculty and administrators to developing student leadership skills"(Report of the Evaluation Team, 1998, p. 10).

Important inroads have been made, but as one dean said, "The institution has just scratched the surface."

University of Washington. Throughout the 1990s, the Seattle campus of the University of Washington, with more than twenty-five thousand undergraduate students and ten thousand graduate students, took important steps to revitalize undergraduate education and create a dynamic environment for its students. These steps exhibit the administration's leadership in bringing significant change to the campus.

The administration created the Office of Undergraduate Education in 1992 to coordinate undergraduate programs campuswide. Through the efforts of this office and other departments, the university began to offer students expanded opportunities and experiences, among them undergraduate research, with an emphasis on learning.

About the same time, the Carlson Office (later renamed the Carlson Center) was created with funds from a generous donation to the university. The original mission of the center was, among other things, to promote, organize, and support opportunities for the university's undergraduates to become actively engaged in experiential learning through community service work (http://www.washington.edu/students/carlson/mission.html). Three years later, the scope of these activities was broadened to include undergraduate research.

In 1995 the president, Richard L. McCormick, reviewed the university's programs to identify new initiatives. Undergraduate research emerged as politically and educationally important, and in a public address, he declared undergraduate research as one of the university's high priorities. Although the mandate was unfunded, it stimulated institutional conversation about ways to shift the emphasis from teaching to learning and to develop research opportunities for students. Several programs were developed as a result of the speech.

In autumn 1995, the Undergraduate Research Program (URP) was established to support students seeking opportunities to get involved in research and to assist faculty in all fields who wished to include undergraduates in their work. URP, with a part-time director and small staff, maintains a Web site that includes an extensive list of research opportunities at the university and beyond, information for faculty on incorporating undergraduates into their work, advice for students on getting started in research, and recognition of students' research accomplishments. URP also organizes the annual Undergraduate Research Symposium and offers assistance to students preparing to present their work at the symposium or in other professional settings.

The Undergraduate Research Symposium gives students the chance to showcase their research projects that build on and enrich faculty work across the disciplines. Students, faculty, and the community have the opportunity to discuss cutting-edge research topics and to examine the connection between research and education. It promotes the undergraduate research enterprise by providing information and examples for students not yet involved in research.

Also in 1995, Bill and Melinda Gates established the Mary Gates Endowment for Students in memory of Bill's mother, the university's longest-serving regent. It is significant that following deep discussions involving faculty and administrators on the needs of the university, the proposal to the Gates family requested funds to foster the development of independent learners and community leaders. In 1999, the Bill and Melinda Gates Foundation added to the endowment, and the annual proceeds are dedicated exclusively to students.

The Gates endowment funds the Mary Gates Scholars program, which supports students each year to do undergraduate research with faculty mentors. Students receive a generous stipend each quarter to allow them to do research without having to hold outside jobs. Students apply for the Mary Gates Scholarships by writing essays about what they expect to learn from the research experience. The deans and a faculty committee evaluate the essays and decide the awards.

The university started the Summer Undergraduate Research Program (SURP) to enhance the undergraduate experience and to challenge the bright students the university recruited from high school on space grant scholarships. SURP allowed these students to do research the summer before they matriculated into the university. Within four years, program participation expanded beyond the space grant program and more than tripled with additional funding from the provost and the Mary Gates Endowment.

The Tools for Transformation program provided incentive for departments to apply for one-time funding of $50,000 to $100,000 to respond to new challenges and to remove impediments to change (http://www.washington.edu/change/proposals). Some of the funded proposals have been student-focused, including research, curriculum transformation, and expansion of service-learning experiences.

The students are beginning to reflect the undergraduate research culture. A group has formed the Undergraduate Research Society (URS) to advertise research positions among students and to provide advice on applying for a research position. The URS meetings provide a forum for students to present their research, discuss current issues in research, and help each other refine their presentations and publications. Within a year of its formation, URS had over 50 members and was one of the fastest growing student organizations on campus.

In October 1998, the University of Washington reported to the state's Higher Education Coordinating Board on state-mandated accountability targets that more than 22 percent of its undergraduates report a research experience with a faculty member. According to Dean of Undergraduate Education Frederick L. Campbell, the university would like to set a goal for every student to have some kind of experiential learning. "It should be a hallmark of the place," he said.

Success has engendered success at the institution, and it is changing its culture to better emphasize undergraduate education in general and undergraduate research and experiential learning in particular. Faculty and administrators are feeling pressure from students who now demand more of these opportunities. In response, the institution has raised funds specifically restricted to the enhancement of undergraduate education. It has also undertaken such simple, low-cost steps as creating a Web site to advertise faculty projects to students. Because of increased student interest, the competition for available positions is greater, and as a result, the quality of the experiences is improving. A faculty member commented, "The students are raising the bar for each other. They are seeing what is possible, and they are going for more. Faculty expectations are higher. We are all learning what can be done, and it is impressive."

Massachusetts Institute of Technology. Undergraduate research permeates the MIT environment. The institute's select undergraduate student body numbers close to forty-four hundred, with over fifty-five hundred graduate students and more than nine hundred faculty. Students are encouraged to get involved in research from the very start.

In 1969, stimulated by a speech by Edwin Land, head of Polaroid, Dean Margaret MacVicar, with the support and encouragement of President Paul Gray, founded the Undergraduate Research Opportunities Program (UROP) to invite and encourage students to become part of the research mission of the institute. UROP at MIT, the first undergraduate research program in the country, has become the model for similar programs at many other universities.

UROP is a clearinghouse for student-faculty collaborations in all the research efforts represented at MIT. Any student can do research through UROP, and they often begin to seek research experiences in the first term of their freshman year. Although students usually join a faculty member's project, they also may design their own projects and recruit faculty to advise them. They work during academic terms and summer. Students may receive pay or academic credit. Occasionally students volunteering to work in a research group receive neither pay nor credit. Students work on campus or at other MIT venues such as Lincoln Laboratory.

About 80 percent of MIT students do at least one UROP project before they graduate, sometimes starting out by doing routine tasks in support of the work of faculty and graduate students. Close to 50 percent of all students do more than one UROP project. When they continue doing research, students often take on increasingly sophisticated and challenging projects. About 20 percent become authors or coauthors of articles in the refereed literature, a measure of the level of research they undertake and of their contributions to the body of knowledge.

Faculty are extremely enthusiastic about and proud of UROP, and more than 45 percent of them participate in the program each year. They describe MIT's focus on students and the abundant undergraduate research opportunities as the essence of the institute. Increasingly, junior faculty attribute their own undergraduate research experiences with setting them on their career paths through graduate school and into academe, and they enthusiastically recruit students to work with them. Sometimes they launch their research programs with undergraduates before they have graduate students with whom to work. However, some assistant professors said that their senior colleagues counseled them to avoid working with undergraduates at this point in their careers.

The UROP staff, 2.5 FTEs, provides infrastructure for the program under the direction of the dean for undergraduate research, who sets UROP policy. The staff advertises the program and holds information sessions for prospective participants. They manage the application process, which consists of a research proposal and a budget. They also communicate program guidelines and goals to the students and faculty, review student proposals, recommend hourly wage levels, and award funding when appropriate. The staff evaluate the program as well as student and faculty experiences through required feedback from mentors and students. Because of the small number of staff, UROP has not yet sponsored a symposium or poster session; however, some departments coordinate such events.

UROP developed a research mentor program in 1993 to take advantage of the "independent activities period" held in January. The program links undergraduates who have never done a UROP project with experienced UROP students who serve as peer mentors. The purpose of the program is to help prepare students to do research and to give upper-class students mentoring experience.

Undergraduate research is ubiquitous at MIT. It pervades the culture, promotes educational growth for its students, and provides the rich opportunities students seek when they choose a university. A new generation of faculty who were undergraduate researchers themselves is beginning to deepen the culture even further. The administration cites the importance and value of UROP to the institute and its contribution to MIT's world leadership in research and education.

California Institute of Technology. Caltech is a small private research institute with a select undergraduate student body of about 900; graduate students number 1,100 and faculty, close to 350. The institute comprises six academic divisions, and it manages the National Aeronautics Space Administration's Jet Propulsion Laboratory (JPL) as a nonacademic division. Undergraduate research is deeply imbedded in the academic culture.

Students are steeped in the research environment, and there are several mechanisms by which they can do research. They may do research for academic credit, or faculty may hire them to work in their laboratories. The students themselves publish the *Undergraduate Research Opportunities Handbook* to allow faculty, research fellows, and postdoctoral and graduate students to advertise projects on which undergraduates might work. Opportunities for off-campus research are readily available on the Web sites of the Student-Faculty Programs Office and the Career Development Center. Close to 60 percent of Caltech students report having done research by the time they graduate.

The Summer Undergraduate Research Fellowships (SURF) provides opportunities for more than one-third of the eligible (rising sophomores, juniors, and seniors) Caltech students to do research under the mentorship of Caltech faculty, JPL technical staff, or with faculty at other universities in the United States and abroad. In addition, more than a hundred students from colleges and universities worldwide participate in SURF at Caltech each year.

Founded in 1979 by then-professor of chemical engineering Fred Shair, SURF is a microcosm of the grant-seeking process. Students collaborate with potential mentors to write research proposals, which are reviewed by a faculty committee that recommends awards. Students carry out the work during a ten-week summer period. Any student who wants to do research can find an opportunity in a variety of fields. The benchmark for a SURF project is the potential for publication, and about 20 percent of SURF students coauthor articles in the refereed literature, present at conferences, or contribute to significant reports. As with any fellowship, students receive a stipend; the 2002 stipend was $5,000.

Because science not reported is essentially science not done, SURF places strong emphasis on communication. Students are required to submit technical papers at the conclusion of the program. They also give oral presentations at SURF seminar day, a symposium modeled on a professional technical meeting. Two donors endowed prizes for the best technical papers and oral presentations to stimulate students to develop excellent technical communication skills. A group of enterprising students developed the *Caltech Undergraduate Research Journal* to showcase undergraduate research in an interesting, readable publication intelligible to any undergraduate. The journal appears on-line and in print.

The SURF program sponsors a wealth of enrichment activities throughout the summer to enhance the research experience. These activities include weekly research seminars given by faculty and presented in a manner accessible to students at all levels in all disciplines. Weekly professional development workshops help students consider their short-term career decisions in the context of long-term life and career goals. Each week during the summer, small groups of students have supper with two or three faculty at local restaurants to promote informal interaction and conversation.

The SURF program raises close to $1 million annually to support student stipends from multiple sources, including endowment, annual gifts from individuals, corporations, and private foundations. These funds are used to match faculty contributions to their students' stipends.

Nearly 60 percent of Caltech science and engineering faculty mentor SURF students each summer. Faculty members also volunteer to review proposals, read final reports, and evaluate oral presentations. SURF depends on the participation of the campus community, and faculty's willingness to support the program in this way is a strong testimony to the value they place on the program.

SURF is the primary program in an array of undergraduate research programs administered by the Student-Faculty Programs Office staffed by three FTEs. Other programs include Minority Undergraduate Research Fellowships for non-Caltech underrepresented students; Axline SURF for a select group of incoming freshmen; and Beckman Scholars for top biology and chemistry students. Students admitted to the auxiliary programs fully participate in SURF.

The Western Association of Schools and Colleges reaccredited Caltech in 1998. The self-study addressed four specific areas, one of them undergraduate research. In their final report to the institute, the visiting team stated, "By all indications the SURF program has been tremendously successful" (1998, p. 73).

Undergraduate research is pervasive at Caltech, and, as President David Baltimore commented, SURF is "one of the jewels in Caltech's crown." Most students choose Caltech because of the opportunities to do research, and faculty expect to involve them in their projects. Students often cite their SURF experiences as among the best of their undergraduate careers. The institute benefits as the students and faculty reap advantages in a culture strongly supportive and encouraging of undergraduate research.

Summary

Research is the coin of the realm at many research universities, and these institutions enhance undergraduate education by including students as intellectual partners in the research enterprise. Undergraduate research in these schools is above all an educational opportunity for students, although sometimes students make significant contributions, become coauthors of articles in the refereed literature, or help junior faculty to launch their research programs.

Undergraduate research makes the transition from one level of education to the next more efficient and seamless, finding out what it is like to be a graduate student. Another benefit is that graduate students and postdoctoral candidates develop mentoring skills they will need as they move into their careers.

Students become members of the community of researchers and scholars as they collaborate with faculty mentors and other researchers. Students sink their roots in the culture of their fields, including the ethics of the discipline. The relationships formed between mentors and protégés often continue as students progress through graduate school or begin their careers.

The research universities have been criticized by the public and the media for emphasizing research over teaching, and undergraduate research can be one of the antidotes to that allegation. The tutorial interaction between mentor and student around a problem of mutual interest is an ideal bridge on the teaching-research continuum. Most students learn best through hands-on exploration of new problems as they apply knowledge gained in the classroom to real-world questions.

Several universities have developed a culture of undergraduate research that pervades the institution and includes the major campus constituencies of faculty, students, and administration. In these institutions, the administration has articulated a vision of undergraduate research as an important component of undergraduate education and has taken steps to bring change to the campus. In discussions about undergraduate research, faculty exhibit evidence of institutional conversation about the issues and have a common understanding of what constitutes undergraduate research. Students are aware of research opportunities available to them. The culture of undergraduate research influences education throughout the institution.

The four institutions described in this chapter have developed strong undergraduate research cultures. Rutgers and the University of Washington, as large public institutions, have addressed the issues that arise from their size and complexity, including vastly diverse student bodies with widely varying needs. These two institutions have brought about significant change and positioned themselves to achieve the goal of including increasingly higher percentages of their undergraduates in research.

Caltech and MIT have cultivated the undergraduate research culture over a long period. These institutions have much smaller, highly select student bodies. The low student-faculty ratio allows any student to participate in research, and most students have a research experience by the time they graduate. Most faculty mentor undergraduates. The culture is so deeply imbedded that there is little need for institutional conversation because all members of the community have a common knowledge of the opportunities and benefits for students, faculty, and the institution as a whole.

These four universities have developed cultures of undergraduate research by dint of creativity and innovation. Undergraduate research opportunities are continuously evolving through diligent and persistent effort supported by an established infrastructure. Each institution can serve as a model of how undergraduate research can become an integral part of undergraduate education.

The Association of American Universities supported a pilot study of undergraduate research at six research universities undertaken during 2000. I thank Nils Hasselmo and the members of the K–16 Task Force for their support and encouragement.

I also thank the two hundred administrators, faculty, and students whom I interviewed at the research universities for giving their time to this project and for sharing their experiences and wisdom.

References

Boyer Commission on Educating Undergraduates in the Research University, S. S. Kenny (chair). *Reinventing Undergraduate Education: A Blueprint for America's Research Universities.* State University of New York–Stony Brook, 1998.

Boyer, E. *College: The Undergraduate Experience in America.* New York: Harper & Row, 1987.

Boyer, E. *Scholarship Reconsidered.* Princeton, N.J.: Princeton University Press, 1990.

Grassmuck, K. "Moving Toward the 21st Century: Some Research Universities Contemplate Sweeping Changes Ranging from Management and Tenure to Teaching Methods." *Chronicle of Higher Education, 37,* A1, A29–31, Sept. 12, 1990.

Nagda, B. A., and others. "Undergraduate Student-Faculty Research Partnerships Affect Student Retention." *Review of Higher Education,* 1998, 22(1), 55–72.

Report of the Evaluation Team to the Faculty, Administration, Trustees, and Students of Rutgers, The State University of New Jersey, Accreditation Review Commission on Higher Education Middle States Association of Colleges and Schools. Philadelphia: Middle States Association of Colleges and Schools, March 29-April 1, 1998.

"Transforming the State Role in Undergraduate Education." *Chronicle of Higher Education,* 1986, 32(22), 13–18.

Western Association of Schools and Colleges Accrediting Commission for Senior Colleges and Universities. Visiting Committee Report to the California Institute of Technology, Oct. 12–15, 1998.

CAROLYN ASH MERKEL directs the Student-Faculty Programs at the California Institute of Technology. Each year about 350 students participate in the institute's SURF program. Merkel and Shenda Baker coauthored the Council on Undergraduate Research's How to Mentor Undergraduate Researchers *(2002).*

4

As with research universities, primarily undergraduate institutions also feel the imperative to exercise hands-on learning. "Students first!" should be the motto of these colleges and universities. But how should they navigate the political waters?

A Research-Across-the-Curriculum Movement

Mitchell R. Malachowski

Predominantly undergraduate institutions (PUIs) are in a state of flux. One obvious change greatly affecting these institutions is the expectation that faculty be engaged in original scholarship that leads to publishable results. Although these institutions generally retain a commitment to students as their primary mission, a research mind-set has taken hold at many institutions, as evidenced by a gradual shift in the allocation of faculty time and resources toward supporting more scholarship. Jacobson (1992) refers to this as "institutional drift" where faculty at non-Ph.D. institutions emulate the work habits of faculty at Ph.D.-granting institutions.

At the same time that faculty respond to internal pressures to become more involved in scholarship, numerous external calls are being made for them to shift more emphasis toward students and less time toward their scholarly interests. As well as calls to shift the emphasis on how faculty spend their time, there are also expectations for them to serve as conduits for more active learning experiences for students. Service learning, internships, group learning activities, and the use of advanced technologies have all been used to help shift many institutions' emphasis from teaching to learning. As a result of these movements, there are numerous initiatives on campuses designed to enhance student learning or as a means of faculty development.

Many voices have discussed the need to move to a learning paradigm whose goals include creating environments and experiences that help students discover and construct knowledge for themselves and to make them members of communities of learners. Although many examples of how this can be done have been described, a powerful process that is not frequently discussed is involving students in faculty research projects. An experience where a faculty member engages a student in an important project and that includes a committed mentoring component may be one of the best models of the learning paradigm that currently exists. Therefore, it is time that we consider a research-across-the-curriculum movement. In doing so, we need to rethink our motivations for doing scholarship and include the involvement between students and faculty as being one of the major impetuses for research at PUIs.

The Nature of Research at Predominantly Undergraduate Institutions

We should begin by considering why faculty at PUIs do research. As with any activity that is undertaken, it must be asked how the increase in faculty scholarship affects student learning. However, of the many problems in trying to assess the effect of research activities on student learning is that scholarship takes many different forms. For example, Boyer (1990) has described four types of scholarship: the scholarships of discovery, application, integration, and teaching. These categories are helpful in defining what we do. However, other categories may be more helpful in assessing the effects of research on the overall student learning environment. Therefore, let us consider a few of the reasons frequently given in support of research at PUIs. Research is said to provide the following benefits: allowing faculty to make contributions to their academic field, keeping faculty intellectually vigorous, enhancing the quality of classroom teaching, and engaging students in original scholarship.

Let me address these four categories. Certainly faculty at PUIs make advances in their discipline, and their research results are meaningful. We should be scholars, and we should stay engaged with and be capable of contributing to our disciplines. Nevertheless, undergraduate research is not the most efficient way to get results because competing with faculty at research universities is usually a losing battle. Therefore, if research results are the prime motivation, the work should probably not take place at PUIs unless other benefits flow from it.

As to the second item, I admit that research often keeps us active and enthusiastic, and there is a spillover effect felt throughout our psyches that should not be overlooked. It is also true that doing research allows us to explain better the process of science, and it helps us demonstrate to students the critical eye needed to separate fact from fiction. Nevertheless, these are not principal reasons for doing research, and no funding agency would consider them in assessing the quality of our work.

In reference to the third category, some research feeds directly into teaching activities, but examples of this are infrequent at best. These typically include research performed by those with Ph.D.s in science education or work that probes teaching methods. For the most part, though, results of basic research projects rarely find their way back into the classroom. My own research into the synthesis and catalytic properties of models for met-alloproteins, for example, has little bearing on what I teach in my organic chemistry classes. I also discount the notion that keeping up with the liter-ature, an activity often cited as having direct effects on classroom teaching, is research because the reader is not generating any new information. Rather, it is part of our professional obligations as teachers where we are expected to share with our students the most up-to-date information.

What of the fourth category? Research at PUIs should be original schol-arship that contributes to one's discipline *and* includes undergraduate stu-dents as an integral part of the research program. The second clause is the key: *research should almost always involve students.* The interaction between faculty and students should provide the major impetus for our work. In this context, not all research currently done at PUIs falls under this rubric. Many departments at PUIs do not include students in their research projects, and not all work done by individuals who usually involve students is amenable to this approach. For example, although I routinely involve undergraduates in my chemical research projects, I do not have students working with me in my studies on the history and philosophy of science. Although this work contributes to the history and philosophy of science courses that I occasionally teach, it should be only a minor portion of my efforts because it takes me away from my students. Therefore, research done by a faculty member that does not include students or that does not directly affect one's teaching is of secondary importance at PUIs and can even be detrimental to student learning and institutional quality.

Student-Centered Versus Research-Oriented Approaches to Research

Faculty research is here to stay, so the fundamental question is whether it is possible for individuals, departments, and institutions to be "research active" while retaining their student-oriented approaches. We need to con-sider what effect research has on students and what happens when faculty exclude students from their scholarship. Numerous studies have exam-ined the effects of faculty-student interactions, and some of these studies probed the involvement of students in undergraduate research projects.

Pascarella and Terenzini (1991) showed that faculty who are most acces-sible to students beyond the classroom appear to share an interrelated set of norms, assumptions, and values about the process of teaching, learning, and student development of which frequent contact with students outside of class would seem to be a natural extension. Other studies delineated the positive associations that exist between the amount of nonclass student contact with faculty and such educational outcomes as satisfaction with college, educa-tional aspirations, intellectual and personal development, academic achieve-ment, and persistence in college (Gurin and Epps, 1975; Hearn, 1987; Kuh and others, 1991; Pascarella, 1980, 1985; and Thistlethwaite and Wheeler, 1966).

Astin's extensive longitudinal studies of students and student learning demonstrates that the two most important factors in student cognitive and affective development, satisfaction, and learning are the nature of students' peer groups *and the quality and quantity of their interactions with faculty outside of the classroom* (Astin, 1977, 1993). These studies are the most pertinent ones to this discussion because he surveys the effects of both faculty activities and attitudes toward students. In his work, he probes the dichotomy between faculty who are "research-oriented" and those who are "student-oriented." The differences on student outcomes between these two approaches are striking.

Astin found that the extent to which faculty are student-oriented produces more substantial direct effects on student outcomes than almost any other environmental variable. The strongest positive effects are on a variety of student satisfaction outcomes: faculty rating, quality of instruction, individual support services, general education requirements, opportunities to take interdisciplinary courses, and the overall college experience. The extent to which faculty are student-oriented also has a great influence on academic outcomes: bachelor's-degree attainment, scholarship, self-reported growth in writing skills, preparation for graduate school, and overall academic development. It also has a direct positive effect on a student's decision to major in some field of physical science. Indirect positive effects include a commitment to developing a meaningful philosophy of life and self-reported growth in foreign-language skills, leadership abilities, general knowledge, and public-speaking skills.

On the other hand, if the faculty are strongly research-oriented, student development is negatively affected, including some of the strongest effects of all of the environmental measures used in Astin's study. A strong research orientation has a substantial negative effect on students' satisfaction with the overall quality of instruction and the overall college experience, graduating with honors, college grade-point average, leadership, growth in public-speaking skills, being elected to a student office, tutoring other students, completing the bachelor's degree, and growth in interpersonal skills. Positive effects are found on performance on standardized tests. These results clearly show that there is a substantial institutional price to be paid, in terms of student development, for a strong faculty emphasis on research, whereas having a strongly student-oriented faculty pays rich dividends in the affective and cognitive development of students. Although the faculty and our professions accrue benefits as a result of research activities, it follows from these studies that the principal motivation for research should be its effect on students.

So why do not all faculty engage students in their research? Because it is still uncommon to find undergraduate research in numerous areas at many institutions, either the faculty do not yet recognize the benefits of involving students or they believe that the negative consequences to the faculty out-weigh any positive student outcomes. When asked, the most common reasons given by many faculty for not involving students in their scholarship include the following: the departmental and disciplinary culture does not encourage it, undergraduates are unable to participate in research at a meaningful level, little or no institutional commitment exists for these endeavors, or there is a lack of compensation and resources. Bost (1992) enumerates the obstacles to the involvement of humanities faculty in undergraduate research. In Bost's work, he argues that research requires access to large libraries, undergraduates cannot write or think at the level required, research in the humanities is a solitary enterprise, and students would need years to get acquainted with the research. In addition, many faculty view themselves as teachers, not researchers, and students don't have the necessary time during the academic year. Although I agree with the validity of some of these resistances, nevertheless, the benefits to our students and institutions seem to far outweigh the challenges of including students.

Institutionalizing Undergraduate Research Across Campus

The culture, outlooks, and atmosphere of a given disciplinary area largely shape the resultant activities of its faculty. In relation to the engagement of students in research projects, we can classify the factors responsible for faculty attitudes and behaviors into a number of broad groupings that include cultural issues, student abilities, institutional viewpoints, compensation, and resources. So how could we try to institutionalize undergraduate research in areas where it is not currently common? I am not arguing for more scholarship on any given campus because this is a separate issue. Instead, I am saying that we should find ways to support faculty who are research active in their ongoing work.

We need to consider the places on our campuses where discussions, evaluations, and decisions are made regarding scholarship. Included among these are hiring, promotion and tenure, awards and honors, compensation, internal grants, salary decisions, resource allocation, facilities and research space, and grants and contracts.

Cultural Issues

What is it that differentiates areas where undergraduate research is deeply rooted from those where it is still rare? The choice of whether to involve students in research projects seems to be largely a cultural issue, and we should begin by probing the origins of these cultural outlooks. Certainly the training of students in the natural sciences and the more experimentally oriented social sciences dramatically differs from that in other social science areas and the humanities. Faculty typically learn how to approach and perform research during graduate school. The culture in the natural science areas is one that is dominated by at least two features that are generally less common in many other disciplines. First, research is a collaborative process in the sciences, where the involvement of many hands and viewpoints has become the norm. Second, results are usually obtained by experimentation, and empirical data are used to forge ahead. This contrasts with scholarship in the humanities and many social science fields, where research is a more solitary enterprise and empirical results are neither the norm nor part of the goals of the projects.

Considering the enormous difference in the training and practices of faculty between different areas, that the engagement of undergraduates in research is treated differently in different areas is not surprising. Two options are available to address this issue. First, because the hiring of new faculty has profound effects on a department's culture, faculty should be hired who embrace involving undergraduates in their work. Another approach is to view this issue as an in-service training, one where the benefits of undergraduate research are promoted to new faculty. In this way, some of the resistances to undergraduate research can be chipped away, and the attitudes in those areas can be reshaped. These cultural issues are significant and are a huge challenge to inculcating undergraduate research across our campuses. However, if a university wants to institutionalize undergraduate research, it should either hire faculty who embrace this viewpoint or display for them the beneficial aspects of this approach.

Quality of Student Participation

One of the main arguments against engaging undergraduates in research projects is the belief that they are incapable of participating at a level that allows for their active involvement. Although there are certainly situations where this is true, it is a mistake to exclude all students on these grounds. Faculty at PUIs whose primary research and research methods are inaccessible to students should be encouraged to rethink and redesign one or more of their projects so that results can be obtained with students, and we should exclude projects that cannot be performed with our resources and students. If one buys into this approach, all faculty can structure their projects to include undergraduates in their work.

Some faculty question whether meaningful results and publications can result from student work and student participation or whether student participation would hinder the faculty to such an extent that the product would suffer. There are ways to structure projects in all disciplines so that they are accessible to student participation. As examples, Dunning (1994) has had positive experiences with undergraduate research projects in the fine arts. He compares his approach with that used in social science research in that a fine arts research curriculum includes an introduction to basic survey-level knowledge, an evaluation of various artistic methods, and a more fine-tuned study of the students' own experiences, which is manifested through final projects. He argues that although the terminology may differ from discipline to discipline, the basic questioning process that underlies research across disciplines is remarkably similar.

Uffelman (1995) has described a successful project he has undertaken with undergraduates that involves research into Victorian literature. He points out that faculty and undergraduates in the humanities can work together on collaborative research when the projects are reasonably well defined and the college supports them in tangible ways. Furthermore, the faculty member must be committed to seeing the research project as an opportunity to teach students as well as do research.

In my own experience, students have helped by doing background readings and investigations for my humanities-based work in the history and philosophy of science. Specifically, we were looking at the role of alchemy in the evolution of eighteenth-century chemical thought. The students did considerable investigations of the literature and much of the background readings and pursued leads that we uncovered. Although the methods may differ, the ability of the students and the expectations placed on them were comparable to those in my chemistry research projects. There are numerous projects in all areas where students can contribute and flourish if the goals of the project are defined so that undergraduate student development and student learning are identified as an integral goal of faculty research. This is the heart of the issue. Student outcomes have to be considered central to our research activities.

Planning and Policy Issues

Typically, an institution has many opportunities to integrate undergraduate research into its programs. Most universities have a strategic long-range plan and use it as the foundation for decision making. Just as universities develop and rely on such plans, departments should also develop their own strategic long-range plans for planning and assessment purposes. Priorities should be made explicit in these documents, and independent studies and research activities should be a part of the academic component. A departmental long-range plan can help the department target specific goals and act in unison. In addition, it can serve as the foundation for budget requests, facilities planning, curricular changes, and external grant submissions. These plans transmit signals to other departments that student-centered research activities are important. The plan would be of considerable utility if the rationale for student-centered research was included.

Rank-and-tenure committees send messages about the relative importance of student-based scholarship. How much relative importance does a particular committee place on scholarship? Scholarship that involves students? Publications? Publications with students? We need to keep in mind that most rank-and-tenure committees are faculty bodies, so it is a group of our own who make these determinations.

The type of institution influences the relative value placed on research, teaching, and service. In a research institution, the successful obtaining of contracts and grants may be paramount, but in some departments at PUIs, research activities can be viewed negatively. At my institution (University of San Diego), the primary determinant of salary increases, promotion, and tenure is quality teaching, even though scholarly or professional activities are also expected and supported. Our university rank-and-tenure document enumerates the many kinds of activities that constitute teaching, service, and scholarship; most important is the emphasis placed on each component of the policy because this is critical in defining how each of us spends our time. What if the environment at an institution (or department) is hostile to research? What then? Reshaping a rank-and-tenure policy is a painful and laborious process, but individual departments can often interpret the document in a way that places a greater emphasis on undergraduate research activities. Typically, rank-and-tenure policies include teaching, professional activities, and service to the institution. The beauty of under-graduate research is that it can be portrayed as fitting into any of these cat-egories, and faculty can justify their student research work in the manner that best suits institutional priorities. Thus, while attempting to change the campus ethos to embrace undergraduate research, faculty can also portray their activities as either teaching or service oriented.

We also can have a direct effect by serving on and addressing these issues with our own rank-and-tenure committees. Campuses need advocates for these efforts, and these advocates need to be involved in the central argu-ments that define our campuses. What better place for this to happen than in evaluations of faculty?

Many campuses have merit pay processes where faculty are evaluated on their performances each year. Most department chairs and deans do not simply count publications and use this number as their assessment of fac-ulty scholarship. But what do they do? Do they consider research that includes students to be more meaningful and more noteworthy than work done individually or off campus? In my experiences, some departments rec-ognize the distinction, but many departments do not, and I would guess that most deans do not factor it in when making their recommendations. The reward systems related to rank, tenure, and merit pay should recognize student-based research activities as central to our missions.

Compensation and Workload

Another area to consider when trying to institutionalize undergraduate research is whether appropriate compensation is offered for supervising this work. Most faculty work under an archaic teaching-load system rather than a workload system, so it is not the norm for faculty to receive teaching credit for supervising undergraduate research projects. The lack of compensation is one of the primary reasons many faculty will not supervise undergraduate research. In this respect, it would be burdensome for faculty to take on undergraduates in their projects because that essentially would amount to a teaching overload. If this issue is not addressed and modifications made, faculty will probably fight a losing battle.

So why do some faculty supervise undergraduates as a fairly routine part of their approach to scholarship? In my department, we added a course called Research Methods, which provides a faculty member some compensation every five years or so. This method of getting credit for research-related experiences was instituted because there was no mechanism to negotiate teaching credit for undergraduate research, even though our students pay for the units that they receive. Some schools have been able to institute direct credit. For example, some give one course reassigned time for every twelve students a faculty member worked with, and faculty are able to bank credit over a few years. Although most are still not properly compensated, many faculty continue to offer undergraduate research opportunities to students because of the positive benefits that students receive from these experiences.

Contrast this situation to what is found for internships. At my institution, many departments offer internships as courses. Faculty who teach the class receive credit for teaching. Internships certainly have been legitimated, and many faculty are now interested in internships and clamor to supervise them. Consider what could happen if independent study or undergraduate research were handled in a similar way, that is, if faculty received teaching credit for supervising projects. First, a message would be sent that these are legitimate offerings and that the university believes in them and gives them its seal of approval. Second, faculty would receive credit for work that they now do voluntarily. And third, the carrot of receiving teaching credit for these offerings might induce other faculty to consider supervising undergraduate research because their time would be compensated. Universities send signals as to what is important for students through their curricular requirements and offerings and to faculty by how they assess and compensate them. Faculty who supervise undergraduate research should be compensated commensurate with that provided for supervising internships.

Resources

Resources also need to be made available to counteract the cultural and attitudinal barriers that prevent faculty from engaging students. Such resources already exist on many campuses. Internal research grants are one possibility. Decisions regarding these grants are frequently made by faculty committees, and they should be lobbied to ensure that they understand the importance of including students in faculty scholarship. The involvement of students puts research of this kind on a higher plane and, therefore, should be encouraged and supported at a higher level. In addition, all faculty could be encouraged to build into their external grant proposals opportunities to remain on campus and engage students in their work as one way of reshaping our scholarship.

Other resources could also be used for these purposes. Summer stipends for students and faculty could be supplied, free on-campus summer housing could be provided to students involved in summer research projects, student research grants could support part of the students' work, or travel funds could be supplied to send students to professional meetings. Funding for these initiatives could come from the overhead from external grants or from other sources tied to existing research activities on a campus. As has been done at several institutions, one goal could be to make undergraduate research activities a line item in an institution's budget.

Justifications and Public Relations

Research can be an expensive endeavor in terms of time and resources expended. At most PUIs, research must be sold to the administration as a tool for student learning and not simply as a faculty activity. Packaged in this way, research meshes well with institutional goals. For example, I would strongly suggest that faculty tie requests for equipment to pedagogical initiatives. The National Science Foundation (NSF) Instrumentation Laboratory Improvement program is a prime example of how to best do this because NSF insists on justifications based on student usage of the equipment.

Working on strategic long-range plans and rank-and-tenure documents are not the only ways to make inroads. Although no one wants to spend valuable time describing what seems to be obvious, it is useful to continually educate administrators about departmental accomplishments, aspirations, and needs. Our biology department, for instance, has been extremely effective at showcasing research by conducting open houses and inviting the president, provost, and deans to attend. Posters of student research projects are also a compelling way to engender support for research efforts.

Outside "experts" are often granted more credibility than experts from within an institution. We have seen that outside consultants can provide a tremendous source of momentum for change, so we should use this resource to our advantage. Therefore, I would recommend an external review of each department every five years or so. Critical to the entire process is who has control over choosing the consultants because the entire tone of the visit and the report can be shaped by the choice of the visiting team.

Another approach may be to develop a consistent message between cognate departments in the sciences or even with other colleagues such as those in fine arts. I am always surprised by the similarity in the problems of these two seemingly different groups. Issues such as the proper credit for teaching laboratories, credit for independent studies, safety issues, costly replacement of equipment, renovations, and the like bind these areas together in ways that are not often discussed. For example, encouraging fine arts faculty to send some of their students to one of the National Conferences on Undergraduate Research (NCUR) can serve as the starting point of a discussion on student research activities.

My perception is that departments who retain contact with alumni demonstrate that they believe in a caring, supportive environment. Clever departments use their alumni's expertise to deliver seminars, serve on departmental boards, or donate time and money to departmental interest. In the examples where we have heard directly from alumni about the attributes of a department, especially instruction and research, we have listened attentively and learned a great deal. In a time of great interest in outcome-based assessment, this information is invaluable. The alumni who attribute some of their success to their research experiences can powerfully influence an institution's decision makers.

Structure of Programs

A number of models exist for involving undergraduates in faculty research, with the organization of these programs tending to fall into one of two groups. The most common is an individual faculty- or departmentally-based model where the framework of engagement between students and faculty is left to the discretion of the faculty within an individual department. These programs typically were started in an area where scholarship particularly was amenable to student involvement or where the culture supported it. For example, in the natural sciences, student-faculty research is a natural outgrowth of laboratory courses where students and faculty have a close one-on-one working relationship. These grassroots programs are usually run within departments, with norms handled either individually or using departmental expectations.

Individual faculty or departmental models take on a variety of forms as a result of differing motivations for the program. The most common scenario is for individual faculty to select students whose work they are familiar with, or faculty are approached by students. There is a certain haphazardness to this process because it is dependent mainly on established relationships. Alternatively, some departments require all students to engage in a research project because the research experiences are considered essential to the goals of the department. In most cases, the traditional curriculum is followed, and research is done during the junior or senior year (or both). Occasionally, however, programs are more progressive in nature where the curriculum is restructured to build steadily and systematically toward a formal research experience in the upper division; many of these programs require all students to do research. Curricular reform may be needed to properly prepare students for their research experiences, but there are considerable challenges in undertaking both curricular and research reforms simultaneously.

Generally, little collegewide oversight and varying degrees of institutional support exist for these programs. The benefits of this arrangement are that the programs can be tailored to mesh with the research methods of the area, and they allow for nearly complete local control. These departmentally based programs have many positive features but at the same time can lead to vastly different modes of faculty behavior across a campus. This can lead to problems in generating collective expectations across campus and confusion in evaluating faculty from other departments.

The second model is the campuswide, research-across-the-curriculum program. Frequently these programs evolve from a departmentally based program when a critical mass of departments has embraced undergraduate research or when a new dean or provost has it as part of an agenda. An institution wishing to design such a program would probably find it useful to first appoint a faculty committee to consider how to design the program.

Campuswide programs usually have an office of undergraduate research and an administrator who oversees and encourages activities throughout campus. Students enter the program either through interactions with individual faculty or by application to the central office, which then helps students connect with a professor. In these programs, admission may be open to all interested students, but frequently there is a minimum grade-point average required, or the program is limited to honors students only. Considerable thought should go into who will be involved in this activity before the program is put in place. The central office handles many of the administrative activities, and in addition, students and faculty commonly can apply for travel grants, summer support, supplies, and equipment. The office is often supported by a research advisory committee of faculty from across the college. A local undergraduate research symposium is frequently part of the efforts of the central office, as is a journal of undergraduate research (often with student editors).

So what would a successful research-across-the-campus program look like? First, faculty would support it across the campus and mesh well with departmental and institutional goals. These goals would be integrated into rank-and-tenure documents, faculty workloads, and resource allocation. Successful programs would have faculty champions, and the director of the program would be a faculty member. The role of the administration would be to support the program physically and psychologically and to find ways to sustain it with external grants and internal monies. The office of undergraduate research would have its own budget line, would give competitive grants to faculty and students, would publicize the achievements of the students, and would assist students and faculty in preparing for conferences. Its goal would be to help create a thriving community of scholars in every department who share their accomplishments with each other and with colleagues outside the university.

Conclusions

The encouragement of research-oriented scholarship at many PUIs is moving our campuses further and further from their own ideals and missions. As the level of scholarship grows at these institutions, the undergraduate institutions run the risk of becoming more and more similar to research universities. PUIs, or even individual departments, where faculty are engaged in scholarship that does not involve students are closer to being the functional equivalent of research universities than we would like to admit. It is essential that faculty embrace an undergraduate research-across-the-curriculum approach to scholarship because faculty members' research orientations can reflect not only how they spend their time but also their personal goals and values and their interest in and accessibility to students.

To embrace a research-across-the curriculum movement, measures need to be taken to ensure that undergraduate research and its outcomes receive more prestige on our campuses. In the absence of a general agreement that these are important activities, many of the other recommendations will not bear fruit. As a first step, the virtues of undergraduate research need to be promulgated. After a great appreciation of undergraduate research is achieved, inroads then could be made toward institutionalizing undergraduate research into areas that do not currently embrace these activities. For example, sending students to research conferences, publicizing their achievements, starting a journal of undergraduate research, or holding research conferences on our campuses allow others to see the tremendous positive effect that these activities have on our students. As the benefits to the students become obvious, we then need to work at making sure that the compensation, resources, and recognition for the faculty are in place so that a compelling reason for reshaping professional outlooks and activities can be acted upon. I can envision many benefits to all departments if they embrace these approaches, including greater community, intellectual vitality, and enhanced student development.

The time has come to many PUIs, and the time is rapidly approaching at many others, where the abdication by the faculty of our students' out-of-classroom lives has reached a stage where irreparable harm is being done to our students and institutions in the name of research-oriented scholarship. A successful research-across-the curriculum effort allows us to retain the positive features of faculty scholarship while enhancing our students' learning experiences and our institutional missions.

References

Astin, A. W. *Four Critical Years: Effects of College on Beliefs, Attitudes, and Knowledge.* San Francisco: Jossey-Bass, 1977.

Astin, A. W. *What Matters in College? Four Critical Years Revisited.* San Francisco: Jossey-Bass, 1993.

Bost, D. "Seven Obstacles to Undergraduate Research in the Humanities (and Seven Solutions!)." *Council on Undergraduate Research Newsletter,* 1992, *13*(1), 35.

Boyer, E. *Scholarship Reconsidered: Priorities of the Professoriate.* Princeton, N.J.: Carnegie Foundation for the Advancement of Teaching, 1990.

Dunning, R. W. "Undergraduate Research in the Fine Arts." *Council on Undergraduate Research Quarterly,* 1994, *14*(1), 136–137.

Gurin, P., and Epps, E. *Black Consciousness, Identity, and Achievement.* New York: Wiley, 1975.

Hearn, J. C. "Impacts of Undergraduate Experiences on Aspirations and Plans for Graduate and Professional Education." *Research in Higher Education,* 1987, *27,* 119–141.

Jacobson, R. L. "Professors Who Teach More Are Paid Less, Study Finds." *Chronicle of Higher Education,* Apr. 15, 1992, pp. A17–A18.

Kuh, G., and others. *Involving Colleges.* San Francisco: Jossey-Bass, 1991.

Pascarella, E. T. "Student-Faculty Informal Contact and College Outcomes." *Review of Educational Research,* 1980, *50,* 545–595.

Pascarella, E. T. "Students' Affective Development Within the College Environment." *Journal of Higher Education,* 1985, *56,* 640–662.

Pascarella, E. T., and Terenzini, P. T. *How College Affects Students.* San Francisco: Jossey-Bass, 1991.

Thistlethwaite, D., and Wheeler, N. "Effects of Teaching and Peer Subcultures upon Student Aspirations." *Journal of Educational Psychology,* 1966, *57*(1), 35.

Uffelman, L. K. "Victorian Periodicals: Research Opportunities for Faculty-Undergraduate Research." *Council on Undergraduate Research Quarterly,* 1995, *15*(4), 207.

MITCHELL R. MALACHOWSKI *assumed the presidency of the Council on Undergraduate Research in 2002. He is professor of chemistry at the University of San Diego. An essay he wrote for the* Council on Undergraduate Research Quarterly *on celebrating undergraduate research at the state capital has guided many "Posters on the Hill" events across the nation.*

5

Although undergraduate research may not be considered typical of the community college mission, many two-year colleges have embraced it for hands-on learning and community action projects.

Undergraduate Research at Two-Year Colleges

Jorge A. Perez

"Sleep Deprivation, Circadian Rhythms, and the Use of Caffeine to Prolong Wakefulness"; "What Happened to Brown? The Continuing Impact of Class Structure on American Education"; "Comparison of Oxygen and Carbon Dioxide Levels in Anesthetized Cats Using a Non-Rebreathing Versus a Rebreathing System"; "Stromelysin Upregulation by LPS and TNF-a." Each of these is an undergraduate research project undertaken at an institution of higher education not historically noted for such activity—the two-year college.

The Community College Culture

Community colleges have shown, since the founding of Joliet Junior College in Illinois in 1901, a willingness to embrace innovation. This aspect of the community college culture has allowed these institutions to serve the particular needs of their communities without abandoning their mission. This mission is shaped by the community colleges' commitment to serve the community through open access to comprehensive educational programs, with emphasis on teaching and learning (Vaughan, 2000). Institutions try to accomplish these commitments using strategies that draw on their particular strengths. These efforts can focus on one or more of the following functions or "missions": the collegiate or academic function, the vocational function, economic development, remediation, and community service (Bailey and Averianova, 1999).

Community college faculties have developed numerous strategies to accomplish the collegiate mission of their institutions: learning communities, writing-across-the-curriculum programs, honors programs, and yes, research. As a result of community college faculties' commitment to innovation and their constant efforts to improve the quality of their academic programs, some of them have concluded, generally independent of each other, that their institutions need to provide undergraduate research opportunities to students. Faculty believe that research opportunities not only will enhance students' chances to transfer to a senior college but also will prepare them for the demands of a four-year degree. That is, they see transfer as an important part of the academic function of a community college.

This is a challenging and intriguing proposition, challenging because traditionally research has been seen as a scholarly activity taking place mainly at graduate schools and intriguing because the question that immediately comes to mind is, is it possible to do research at the community college level? And if the answer is yes, the question is, what constitutes research at this level? What are its goals?

Gathering Information

While an American Council on Education Fellow at Pace University in New York, I conducted a study to explore how community colleges are becoming involved in undergraduate research activities and how this involvement can be beneficial to faculty and students as well as to the institutions themselves.

To collect data for this study, I designed a questionnaire addressed to vice presidents or deans for academic affairs and department heads. To avoid confusion or ambiguity, the questionnaire defined undergraduate research at community colleges as all kinds of research that is done by students under the guidance and mentorship of a faculty member. The questionnaire had two parts: the first part was intended for institutions that did not have undergraduate research activities and the second part for those who have implemented them already. This questionnaire was mailed to two hundred community colleges randomly selected from all over the country. A total of forty-seven institutions responded.

The results show that seven, or around 15 percent of community colleges that responded to the survey, are providing research opportunities to their students under the mentorship of faculty members. (While these are not large numbers, the responses do provide a window onto such activity in institutions where one might not expect any to be present.) Fifty-seven percent of these institutions support these activities using internal funds, and the other 43 percent uses grant money (Table 5.1).

The larger percentage shows that community colleges are willing to reallocate their own financial resources to support undergraduate research. It is important to recognize here that these institutions have kept their commitment to undergraduate research even during times of financial constraints.

Undergraduate research at community colleges, as defined by the respondents, may be accomplished through problem-based learning

Table 5.1. Survey Results from Seven Community Colleges That Feature Undergraduate Research

No. of Institutions	% of Respondents	Characteristics
$n = 4$	57	Fund undergraduate research with their own financial resources
$n = 3$	43	Fund undergraduate research with grant money
$n = 5$	71	Administrators consider the quality of faculty as the college strength to do research
$n = 4$	57	Consider the quality of students as the college strength to do research
$n = 2$	29	Reward faculty with released time
$n = 2$	29	Consider undergraduate research a college contribution
$n = 1$	14	Indicate facilities as a strength to do research
$n = 0$	0	Consider elected officials an obstacle to doing undergraduate research
$n = 3$	43	Consider financial resources an external obstacle to doing research
$n = 4$	57	Perceive a correlation between undergraduate research and the college reputation
$n = 2$	29	Believe that special federal or state programs would facilitate undergraduate research

techniques applied to projects in areas such as archeology, psychology, chemistry, biology, mathematics, and social sciences under the guidance of campus faculty. In this sense, the two-year college follows the advice of the Boyer Commission (described in Chapter Two) to institute an inquiry-based learning model. Students may work with experts from local universities, museums, and hospitals. Action-based research, grounded in applying knowledge to a local problem, seems particularly appropriate to the community college mission.

Based on the sample results, of the institutions that do not have undergraduate research, 18 percent indicate that they lack appropriate facilities, and 28 percent lack funds (Table 5.2). Eighty percent noted that it does not fall into the purview of the community college mission. Although faculty may be interested in such research opportunities, the administration sets an institutional tone that discourages such collaborative activity. Even so, a high percentage of these administrators believe that undergraduate research activities would benefit their faculty from a professional perspective. The administrators worry that elected officials or trustees of the college district might view undergraduate research as a diversion from the mission.

Institutional Strengths

Undergraduate research is most likely to occur at institutions that see themselves as having strong students, excellent and motivated faculty, and a transfer tradition. Why are community college faculty willing to serve as

Table 5.2. Survey Results from Forty Community Colleges That Do Not Have Undergraduate Research Programs

No. of Institutions	% of Respondents	Characteristics
$n = 12$	30	Believe that an institutional strength to do research is the college's students
$n = 9$	23	Give facilities as one of the reasons to eventually do undergraduate research
$n = 9$	23	Consider elected officials an obstacle to do undergraduate research
$n = 30$	75	Consider financial resources an external obstacle
$n = 18$	45	Perceive no correlation between undergraduate research and the college reputation
$n = 20$	50	See undergraduate research as a curricular component of an honors program
$n = 18$	45	Consider that undergraduate research would help students become better students
$n = 16$	40	Believe that undergraduate research would motivate students to transfer
$n = 32$	80	Believe that undergraduate research would be an intellectual challenge to students

mentors to students on research projects? Some find it intrinsically motivating, and others are compensated with travel funds, special assistance in grant writing, release time, and merit pay for service. Others note the prestige factor: "To participate with universities in a major federal grant enhances my college's reputation"; it "raises perceptions with participating institutions and their communities who read of our effort in their newsletters"; and "[u]ndergraduate research helps demonstrate that we are attempting to be in the forefront of our professional activities."

What are the perceived benefits of undergraduate research for two-year students? In addition to "learning more about themselves" through research, students enhance their critical thinking skills, and research encourages them to transfer to a senior institution, perhaps a research university. At the two-year college where a thesis is required as a capstone experience, this experience provides a good foundation for continued research at a transfer institution.

The Drawbacks

The administrators' perceptions about the implications of engaging students in research activities are strikingly different between institutions that do and those that do not do research. Research activities do not demand the reallocation of scarce financial resources, according to administrators in the former category, whereas 73 percent feel the opposite would occur if they were to start a research program. Similarly, at colleges with research programs in place, only 14 percent of the administrators consider these activities a burden on an already-busy faculty compared with the 75 percent who feel the same way at those colleges without undergraduate research activities. According to these administrators, undergraduate research activities "might distract faculty who least need to be distracted." And it moves some faculty to "place emphasis upon research as opposed to learning." They also indicate that research activities could distract faculty from the college mission. The general perception at institutions with ongoing research activities is that they do not translate into any drawback to the institution because all activities are "directly related to applied research needed in the workplace."

A possible interpretation of these results is that research has a better chance to occur at institutions where there is a perception, real or not, that faculty are not overburdened. What this situation seems to suggest is that perceived load, rather than real load, is taken as a valid reason not to do research.

Relationship Between Research and an Institution's Reputation

Is there a relationship between research activities and reputation? For institutions that define student research as part of the teaching and learning process, the answer is yes. These institutions often see a synergistic relationship between the school and the community and the school and other institutions of higher education. They note that being a collaborator on a major federal grant enhances the college's reputation, and it signals that the faculty is in the forefront of professional activities. Such activities of students and faculty are highlighted in publications as reputation enhancing.

For colleges without research programs, research is defined as an activity separate from teaching and learning, as characterized in these responses: "The reputation of a community college is more significantly tied to its responsiveness to student and community needs, quality service and programs, and tangible outcomes in degrees, certificates, and constant training than to research"; "we pride ourselves on being a teaching institution, and we have a very good reputation for teaching. Research would not mean much in our community."

To change this perception would require external forces such as a national effort by public agencies or, as one respondent put it, "business and industry interest in applied and technical research." How an institution characterizes research has much to do with its level of activity and success.

Providing a Beacon

Although the number of two-year colleges engaging in undergraduate research is admittedly limited, some of the colleges that do are powerfully engaged in the enterprise. A group of at least fifteen community colleges from Pennsylvania, Massachusetts, New Jersey, New York, and Maryland have organized themselves for several years as the "Beacon Associate Colleges." The main goal of the group is to organize an annual conference to showcase the results of their undergraduate research programs.

The Beacon Steering Committee invites students from the Beacon Associate Colleges and other interested community colleges to submit papers about their research activities. The topics are drawn from eighteen areas of social sciences, natural sciences, humanities, mathematics, and technical fields. The annual publicity to recruit and inform notes that the criteria to evaluate papers include the "quality and originality of research, written work, and oral presentation." Further, "the method and tools of research/analysis" can "vary from discipline to discipline. For example, field work might be part of an anthropology presentation while lab reports might be featured in a scientific or technical paper. All submissions must show the results of research, reflection, and original perspective." Each paper is read and evaluated according to originality and the quality of the research and its results by a group of three faculty members with expertise in the subject. The authors of the three best papers in each field are invited to present at the annual Beacon conference. The conference is funded through a Fund for the Improvement of Post-Secondary Education grant and financial support from the participating colleges. The invitation has become for many students a genuine source of pride because it validates their scholarly efforts.

The Beacon 2000 Conference Program, hosted by SUNY Rockland Community College, included a diverse array of presentations from the allied health and nursing area: "Mental Illness: Real and Underinsured"; from education: "Incentive Reading Programs: Do Incentives Help or Hinder?"; and from philosophy: "Living Up to One's Moral Consciousness: A Study of Socrates and Sharansky."

Undergraduate Research Opportunities at LaGuardia Community College

The Beacon conference provides an opportunity to disseminate results from undergraduate research projects, such as those undertaken at my home institution, LaGuardia Community College in Long Island City. Since 1993, LaGuardia Community College has had an excellent research program, Bridges to the Future, funded by the National Institutes of Health (NIH). The level of research undertaken by the students and the active participation of faculty have made renewal possible at the end of each three-year cycle.

For their participation, students get a "salary" according to the NIH regulations: $5.50 per hour, assuming that they work fifteen hours per week for eight months. Faculty doing research and mentoring three or more students for eight months get three credit-hours per semester in the form of released time or overtime.

Students are recruited into the program based on their academic record and motivation. In fact, motivation to do research is the primary factor in their selection. Mentors recommend students, and the final decision is made by the project director, who is ultimately responsible for the success of the program. According to the director, seasoned mentors take care in their recommendations because they want their students to present quality reports at the closing seminar.

Before the Bridges to the Future program, LaGuardia did not have appropriate facilities to do research. To solve this problem, initially mentors borrowed equipment from senior colleges that was often out of date or redundant. Later, with funding provided by an Instrumentation Laboratory Improvement grant from the National Science Foundation (NSF), the program director obtained an ultraviolet-visible spectrophotometer, an analytical balance, pH meters, and other pieces of equipment. This was the starting point of significant research at LaGuardia. Also, the program developed an Internet laboratory using funding from the Minority Science Engineering Improvement Program program by the U.S. Department of Education. In addition, the CUNY (City University of New York) Research Fund provided the resources to establish a molecular biology laboratory. Later, a private foundation provided additional money to support the program. Because of these new facilities, the LaGuardia Community College Bridges to the Future program is housed in a two-year campus. Other community colleges with Bridges to the Future programs send their students to work in senior colleges.

Student projects have ranged from "Ubiquitin/Proteasome Pathway in Neurodegeneration" to "Molecular Biology of the Human Vomeronasal Organ" and "Systematic Studies of the Characteristic Reactions Between Vanadium and Amino Acids."

The following are some of the advantages that the program provides to the students: the opportunity to work in well-equipped laboratories before transferring to a senior college, a close relationship with a mentor over a long period, advisement opportunities, the chance to work with good role models, and the opportunity to work in a laboratory setting.

Since its inception, the program has served a total of 168 students, with an annual target of 27 to 28 students. Among the 26 participants in the first cohort, 23 were minorities. The combined graduation and transfer rate of the first cohort was 92 percent ($n=24$), with 80 percent of them ($n=19$) transferring to a senior college. Thirteen students earned a bachelor's degree, and six continued in graduate programs. One became a physician, and two are enrolled in a Ph.D. program. The trend with the second cohort is about the same. According to the program director, research activities should be presented to faculty as an activity whose goal is to help students to learn better and to explore their potential, not as an activity that will help the faculty to obtain tenure or promotion. If portrayed otherwise, they might be reluctant to participate out of fear that it could become a requirement for advancing their careers. Community college faculty see themselves as professionals whose primary responsibility is teaching and not research.

Discussion

The results of this study and, in particular, colleges in the Beacon group show that some community college students have the opportunity to participate in undergraduate research activities. At these institutions, administrators consider the excellence of faculty and the strengths of their students as the main reasons that undergraduate research takes place. The high quality of the research work done by students at these institutions and the excellent assessment results at LaGuardia Community College clearly show that research at the community college level invigorates faculty and motivates students to excel.

The support of administrators is critical from a financial perspective because more than half of their colleges use the institutions' own budget to support research. Administrators' comments suggest that undergraduate research is considered a significant and valuable college contribution, which certainly ensures the continuation of these activities.

Answers provided by administrators at institutions without undergraduate research activities indicate that they see their students as not strong enough to do research. However, a significant number of them consider that undergraduate research opportunities would help and motivate students not only to become better students by intellectually challenging them but also to enable them to transfer to senior institutions.

A high percentage of administrators see elected officials as the most serious impediment to open undergraduate research opportunities for students. This position is mostly based on their own understanding of the mission of the community college, which in their opinion does not include the exposure of students to research activities.

Considering that only 5 percent of the administrators participating in this study indicate a lack of interest among faculty to justify the absence of undergraduate research opportunities, we could speculate that research does not take place because of policy decisions at the administrators' level.

Some of these administrators might support undergraduate research at their institutions if there were a strong commitment from the faculty. However, for such faculty initiative to prosper, a greater commitment to undergraduate research from state, federal, and private funding sources is needed. The concrete support to undergraduate research shown by the U.S. Department of Energy, the NIH, and the NSF needs to be emulated by other state and federal governmental agencies. Also needed is a characterization of undergraduate research as integral to teaching and learning. For the two-year college, community-based-action research is also appropriate. What the data suggest is that two-year colleges may be as diverse in their roles and missions as their four-year counterparts, characterized in this volume by primarily undergraduate institutions and research universities.

References

Bailey, T., and Averianova, I. "Multiple Missions of Community Colleges: Conflicting or Complementary?" CCRC Brief, *1*, pp. 1–6. New York: Community College Research Center, Teachers College, May 1999.

Vaughan, G. *The Community College Story*. Washington, D.C.: Community College Press, 2000.

JORGE A. PEREZ *is professor of mathematics and head of the department at LaGuardia Community College, Long Island City, New York. In 1999–2000, he was an American Council on Education Fellow at Pace University, New York. In Summer 2002, he was a visiting scholar at Educational Testing Services in Princeton, New Jersey.*

6

A program was designed to promote interdisciplinary research by undergraduates during the summer. Lessons learned from the first four years of this initiative are described.

Interdisciplinary Research: The NCUR-Lancy Awards

David F. Lancy

In this chapter, I offer a preliminary report of a national program designed to promote undergraduate research. The genesis of this program is marked by considerable serendipity. My father, Leslie E. Lancy, a successful chemical engineer, died in 1996, leaving me trustee of a small family foundation. The only guidance on how to proceed was his track record of philanthropy, primarily in support of students from impoverished backgrounds. I cycled through a variety of directions for the foundation to take, but several factors conspired to focus my attention on undergraduate research. As director of an honors program, which included oversight of an undergraduate research grant program, I was troubled by two nagging issues that occupied my thinking. One, what can we do about the fact that some of our best and brightest students must spend time working at minimum wage jobs to pay for college to the detriment of time devoted to faculty-supervised projects? Two, what are the implications for undergraduates of being enrolled in a Carnegie Foundation-designated "research university?" Does such classification affect undergraduate education? Fortunately, these nagging issues were clarified through discussions with David Peak, a close colleague and physicist, who has been for years among a handful of pioneers in promoting undergraduate research. As one of the founders of the National Conferences on Undergraduate Research (NCUR), Peak helped crystallize the concept of an undergraduate research grant program that honored my father and his interdisciplinary interests—engineering and art collecting—and provided support for deserving and meritorious students.

NCUR is a not-for-profit organization committed to the promotion of undergraduate research and creative activity in all academic disciplines and at all institutions of higher learning (Werner, 2002b). To date, its primary outlet for this endeavor has been an annual conference—inaugurated in 1987—held for three days in the spring on a college or university campus that brings together participants from all across the country. The main function of the conference is to provide undergraduates the opportunity to present their scholarly work in an environment similar to what exists at professional conferences. Faculty and administrators also participate in network sessions to share ideas about undergraduate scholarly activity, focusing on such topics as the establishment and funding of undergraduate research programs, the expansion of undergraduate research to all disciplines, and the introduction of problem-based learning and critical-thinking components of undergraduate research into other college courses. The NCUR annual conference provides a rich and energizing experience for its participants, serves as a valuable conduit for the dissemination of useful information on the role of investigative learning in pre-baccalaureate education, and creates a coherent framework for advancing the theme of research in the undergraduate curriculum.

NCUR, a dynamic organization characterized by a high level of dedicated volunteerism, agreed to a partnership with the Lancy Foundation. Negotiation began in the spring of 1998. Later that year, the details hammered out, a request for proposals was issued. In essence, the request invited institutions of higher education to submit proposals for three years to fund a summer fellowship program, offering a maximum of $50,000 for year one of a project, with $25,000 in succeeding years. Programs were required to have an interdisciplinary character with multiple faculty mentors and a variety of co-curricular activities, including, we hoped, a seminar. Our goals included extending opportunity beyond the "hard" sciences, which we felt were fairly well provided for already. Using an interdisciplinary seminar to anchor the fellowships would add significantly to the learning value of the experience. Grant funds were to be used primarily for student stipends because the program is seen as explicitly relieving students of the need to seek paid summer employment.

The First Four Years: Initial Impressions

At the completion of four rounds of competition, a few generalizations can be drawn. In the first round, 104 proposals were submitted, and the NCUR selection panel found that they divided evenly among predominantly doctoral-, master's- and baccalaureate-level institutions. To ensure representation among institutional types, two proposals from each category were funded. We received proposals from prestigious public and private institutions as well as from smaller, less well-known institutions. Perhaps not surprisingly, in the initial rounds, the preponderance came from the prestigious end of the continuum, schools poised to take advantage of new funding sources. Submissions from very large or very small schools were rare and awards even rarer. The largest universities seem to have difficulty organizing cross-disciplinary collaboration, and very small schools seem to lack the grantsmanship capability.

However, schools were passed over that were deemed to be already well advanced in supporting undergraduate research. Indeed, I have been pleasantly surprised at how many schools, including public institutions, have already accorded undergraduate research a prominent position in undergraduate programming. Yale University, for example, is in the middle of a review of undergraduate education, its first in thirty years; the committee will explore ways in which students can "participate in front-line research" (Branch, 2002). Other schools were passed over that had little or no infrastructure or track record with undergraduate research. That is, we wanted to use the Lancy Foundation funds as fertilization to enrich newly tilled and planted soil rather than scatter it on rocky ground or on already-ripening stalks. Colloquially, we sought the biggest bang for our buck, although, in truth, making this judgment has been far from straightforward. Given the wealth of proposals, we were saddened not to be able to fund more.

Among the highest-ranked proposals, we consistently saw evidence of leadership from the top, including several presidents who made the expansion of undergraduate research a benchmark of their tenure. And we saw consistent evidence of the grassroots effort of a cadre of overworked faculty determined to provide their best and brightest students with hands-on learning opportunities.

Another dimension of variation emerged when we looked at the depth promised in the program. Was the program yearlong? Was there related coursework or a seminar? Was a project publication, Web site, or video anticipated? Were faculty meeting *their* obligations to conduct research and publish as part of this program?

Strong proposals had a clear interdisciplinary focus, a powerful discriminator in our deliberations. That is, we had lots of "good" proposals but far fewer good proposals that also had solved the interdisciplinary problem. Proposers might list a suite of varied disciplines that would be catered for, mostly by picking a varied roster of faculty mentors. But it was much harder to demonstrate any synergy among the disciplines and show how they might work together to solve a problem. Not surprisingly, therefore, the model proposal focuses on ecology. Threatened environments offer rich opportunities for research in the sciences, social sciences, history, and journalism. An obviously related point is that most projects focus on issues of local importance (Werner, 2002b).

The First-Round Awardees

Loyola Marymount University in Los Angeles, designated for our purposes master's level, was one of the first-round awardees. Their project, "The Bellona Wetlands," spearheaded by a faculty member from the Spanish program—Jennifer Eich—focused on a threatened area near campus. The project got under way in 1999 and received continuation funding the following year. I caught up with the team from Loyola Marymount at the NCUR conference April 2000. It was an intellectually and culturally diverse group of students. In total, they made eight presentations at the conference spread over six sessions (Exhibit 6.1). In one session, they showed a videotape record of the project produced by media studies majors. It has become *de rigueur* for grantees to bring a contingent of Lancy fellows to NCUR, and the grants underwrite most of these expenses.

Bowdoin College in Brunswick, Maine, and University of South Dakota–Vermillion also used their grants to support interdisciplinary research with an ecological flavor. Under the leadership of chemist Silvia Ronco, the University of South Dakota project was rooted in the Missouri River and Lewis and Clark's epic journey of exploration. This more eclectic focus allowed them to reach out to a broad array of disciplines that were melded together through a rich menu of field trips (Ronco and Engstrom,

Exhibit 6.1. Loyola Marymount University Portion of NCUR Program, 2000

Environmental Science
> On the Complex History of Human Occupation in the Bellona Wetlands: From the Prehistoric Period to the Present (Environmental Sciences)
>> Adam Nicolai, Loyola Marymount University

> The Bellona Wetlands/Playa Vista Development: A Social Costs-and-Benefits Analysis (Economics)
>> Sharon Lee, Loyola Marymount University

Economics-Environmental
> A Logistic Analysis of Attitudinal Preferences Concerning the Playa Vista/Bellona Wetlands Project in Los Angeles, California (Economics)
>> May To, Loyola Marymount University

Engineering-Civil 1
> The Tidal Flow Gates in the Bellona Wetlands (Civil Engineering)
>> Anthony Podegracz, Loyola Marymount University

> Accumulation of Heavy Metals in the Organisms of the Bellona Wetlands (Los Angeles) (Chemistry)
>> Dana Danielson, Loyola Marymount University

Literature-Psychological Themes
> Fact Versus Fiction: Exploring the Rhetorical Devices Used in the Bellona Wetlands Controversy (Rhetoric and Composition)
>> Kirstin Pesola, Loyola Marymount University

Undergraduate Research Network (URN)-Developing Interdisciplinary Undergraduate Research
> Walking in Someone Else's Shoes: The Possibilities, Perils, and Triumphs of Interdisciplinary Undergraduate Research
>> Jennifer Eich, Loyola Marymount University

2000): to the Yankton, South Dakota, area that included visits to the Lewis and Clark Visitor Center, which sits atop Calumet Bluff; to the South Dakota Fish Hatchery and Aquarium; to the Gavins Point Dam and power plant, one of four major dams in South Dakota that harness the river's energy; a canoe trip down a particularly scenic fifteen-mile stretch of the Missouri River; and a hike up Spirit Mound (located six miles north of Vermillion), one of the landmarks described by Lewis and Clark in their journals. This trip included readings of appropriate excerpts of the Lewis and Clark journals; an airplane ride over the Missouri River and neighboring areas; and a visit to the Sergeant Floyd monument in Sioux City, Iowa, with interpretive insights provided by history professor Kurt Hackemer.

Three more institutions (out of 104 submissions) were awarded grants in 2000, and the first-round awardees were given continuation funding. Jill Singer and colleagues (2000) at Buffalo State seized on the centennial of the Pan American Exposition as a unifying theme for their project. Essentially, students and faculty planned to examine changes in Buffalo—especially in the area of the Frederick Law Olmsted Park that had housed the exposition—and to integrate their work into a unified presentation. Like the Lewis and Clark group, Singer's cohort (including twelve fellows) undertook numerous exploratory field trips to immerse themselves in the landscape and culture of the area.

By the third round, the long odds of getting funded had reduced interest in the fellowship program, and we received only thirty-eight submissions, with few doctoral-level institutions represented. The four awardees included Bridgewater State College in Massachusetts; Saint John's University–College of St. Benedict in Collegeville, Minnesota; Elmhurst College in Illinois; and Central Washington University (CWU) in Ellensburg, Washington. Proposals were tightly scripted and clearly addressed these criteria: the institution showed evidence of leadership and planning for undergraduate research, competent project leadership and a committed team of faculty mentors, a clear seminar program for participants, an interdisciplinary theme with specific scaffolding to ensure that students could be matched with disciplines and projects, a plan for dissemination, a plan for raising funds to continue the summer fellowship program, and that the project would not get lost in a preexisting lush jungle of summer research opportunities for students.

Far and away the most ambitious in this round was the CWU project, led by Jim Cook, "Sustainability in Urban China: Environment, Pollution and Society in Twenty-First Century Beijing," where students and faculty spend time at the East-West Center and in China. This project initially seemed high risk because it required much more support than available through Lancy Foundation funds. Fortunately, supplemental funding was forthcoming. Cook applied for and received National Science Foundation funding to carry on the China-environment project for the next three years. CWU was granted $330,000 to run a "research experience for undergraduates" site in Shanghai one year and in Canton, Chongqing, in the following years. The three remaining awardees also have an ecological focus.

In the most recent round of competition, the decline in the stock market limited us to two awards (out of twenty-eight submissions [Werner, 2002a]), to Luther College in Decorah, Iowa, and the University of Nebraska at Kearney. The Kearney project was considered a model proposal (http://www.unk.edu/acad/gradstudies/PlatteStudies/PlatteStudiesHome.html). The Platte River serves as the focus of the project, and topics range from "Concentrations of Herbicides in the Platte" to "Changing Land Ownership Patterns along the Platte" to "Writers of the Platte River." A "research methods" workshop in the spring will prepare the ten fellows by helping them develop proposals for their summer activity. This will be followed by an interpretive field trip in May. During the eight-week summer research session, a weekly seminar meeting will be held at which students will report on their progress. A number of products are anticipated, including a workshop on campus in the fall and presentations at the spring NCUR.

Conclusions

Programs that support undergraduate research are no longer a novelty. There remains enormous variation in the funds available, however. In my admittedly limited experience, I have encountered schools with intramural funds available for student research and creative activity ranging from $5,000 to well over $1 million per annum. But public institutions are taking advantage of opportunities to piggyback undergraduate research on externally funded research activity, and public and private schools have targeted undergraduate research in their development campaigns. Still, I see an important unmet need for summer research funding. Students must often work during the summer to support themselves. Hence, the prospect of earning while learning is extremely attractive for students and dramatically enhances the university's mission. Admittedly, we have a long way to go because the number of students afforded such opportunities is still a miniscule fraction of the total, but the NCUR-Lancy partnership provides a model that reaches out to students in all disciplines and offers bridges among them.

References

Branch, M. A. "A Fresh Look at the College." *Yale Alumni Magazine,* 2002, *115*(6), 38–43.
Ronco, S., and Engstrom, R. "Retracing the Lewis and Clark Expedition: An Interdisciplinary Undergraduate Research Program at the University of South Dakota." *Council on Undergraduate Research Quarterly,* 2000, *21*(1), 17–21.
Singer, J., and others. "The Centennial Celebration of the Pan-American Exposition: A Research Opportunity for Undergraduates at Buffalo State College." *Council on Undergraduate Research Quarterly,* 2000, *21*(1), 12–16.

Werner, T. C. *A Summary of the First Round of the Second Phase of the NCUR/Lancy Initiative.* Schenectady, N.Y.: Union College, 2002a.

Werner, T. C. "The National Conferences on Undergraduate Research (NCUR): Promotion of Research Across All Disciplines." Paper presented at American Association for the Advancement of Science annual meeting, Boston, Feb. 2002b.

DAVID F. LANCY is trustee of the Alice and Leslie Lancy Foundation and director of honors, Utah State University.

*An anthropologist reflects on his efforts to involve
undergraduates in research and creative endeavors. He
concludes with a set of questions that focus the reader's
attention on creating undergraduate opportunities in
research.*

What One Faculty Member Does to Promote Undergraduate Research

David F. Lancy

I did not set out to organize my professional life to maximize opportunities
for undergraduates to do original research and creative projects, but that
seems to be the result. Certainly the institutional context has influenced my
direction as a researcher and a mentor of undergraduate researchers. As a
faculty member in an anthropology program that extends only to the baccalaureate degree, I work with undergraduates who fill niches normally
occupied by graduate students. In addition, nearly all of our undergraduates work to pay for their schooling, so they are keen to find academically
meaningful job opportunities. Furthermore, our honors program has a tradition of pairing its students with faculty willing to work with undergraduates. In other words, the undergraduate researchers are available and
willing, especially if the research project has a stipend attached. In this
chapter, I relate my experiences on how I have been able to help undergraduates find research opportunities.

The Curriculum and Undergraduate Research Opportunities

I teach a course related to my research called "The Ethnography of
Childhood," which incorporates a required methods component. Students must conduct an ethnography—under my supervision—of a setting where children can be found. The process includes an annotated
bibliography, a proposal, a review of literature, a timeline, and a budget.
The culminating oral presentation of reports is treated as a "conference"
and includes a printed "program." Presentations are carefully rehearsed

to fit within the time constraints and illustrated by slides or transparencies. Some ethnographies evolve into senior projects, and many serve as a springboard to graduate school. In addition to the on-campus presentations, these reports are invariably delivered at both local and national conferences. My responsibility is to share information with students about these dissemination opportunities and to provide small travel subsidies whenever possible.

Our program employs undergraduates as teaching fellows in many of our classes. In addition to fairly routine chores, they are often given the opportunity to prepare and deliver a lecture on a topic in which they have developed expertise. These lecture opportunities reinforce a message delivered often and in many guises, namely that students should strive to actively master the discipline and develop ownership of a piece of it through their original research.

In my role as director of the on-campus anthropology museum, I actively involved students in the creation of its exhibits and multimedia materials. Donors funded internships to provide support of students' work in the museum. Following an apprenticeship model, students work their way up an experiential ladder where, at the top rung, they develop a project that incorporates both the original research on poorly documented or understood artifacts and the creative and challenging tasks of exhibit design, funding, and construction. I am joined by my colleagues in the program in supervising students, but in general, students are the primary owners of the research that results in the exhibitions. These products of undergraduate research see a great deal of traffic due to the school visitation program as well as the walk-in traffic. The increasingly complex tasks asked of these students and the concrete results of their work provide an excellent foundation for a career as museum developer and curator.

As a true Boyerian, I believe in the scholarship of teaching (Boyer, 1990; Boyer Commission on Educating Undergraduates in the Research University, 1998). Not only do I strive to make a science of my teaching, but when appropriate, I disseminate the results. When I saw a gap in pedagogical approaches to address the important anthropological concept of kinship, I worked to develop a game for use in my introductory anthropology class, assisted ably by Dan Call, an undergraduate. The Kin Game was adopted for distribution by the American Anthropological Association (Lancy and Call, 1998). Another curriculum project, "Whose Mummy Is It?" (Lancy and others, 2000), employed during its five-year gestation over twenty undergraduates. They all harvested senior theses, conference presentations, and publications (Andrew, 2000) as well as developing skills in multimedia design, computer animation and graphics, and programming. Typically, I take students on for one semester in a nonpaying, for-credit apprenticeship, using independent study or internship course numbers. If they prove themselves, I hire them.

Faculty Research and Undergraduates

My research focuses on the role of culture in children's development. Writing for a broad audience through both academic professional journals and textbooks has been an important part of my faculty role. Undergraduates have been employed as research assistants on several projects and are paid out of grant funds. I enlist students to assist with searching out and synthesizing critical topics. For example, Jaclyn Emmet (2001) took a piece of my work in progress on the nature of childhood. She produced a fine essay on "The Paradox of Infanticide," which eventually became the focus of her senior honors thesis.

At first glance, it may seem selfish to guide students to work on topics that feed into a faculty member's research agenda. On the contrary, students usually welcome the guidance and close supervision implied by this mutual self-interest. Of course, the faculty member must ensure that the student's original contribution is acknowledged and, indeed, effectively promoted. I treat the students as colleagues and include them as coauthors when the results are published. This is an ethic shared by nearly all of my colleagues. Certainly the archaeologists and physical anthropologists are in the best position to incorporate student researchers in their projects, but several cultural anthropologists employ students as well.

Also in the spirit of Boyer, I conduct continuous and imaginative assessment of my classes to gather information about how and what my students are learning and then to use that evidence to revise the curriculum. The imperative to assess and reflect carries through to my role as honors director, a position where I am constantly involved in evaluating programs from planning to implementation. Of course, I employ students to help in conducting these various assessments and to analyze the results. Supervising students who participate in assessment activities takes extra effort, but the results are noteworthy. I ensure that the students I employ are involved in every step of the operation so that they complete the process with a good sense of how surveys get constructed, how to develop coding schemes for qualitative data, and how to communicate results.

Funding to support undergraduates in these endeavors comes from many sources: college programs, internal and external grants, royalties, and stipends from overload Web-based classes. Because I believe in the importance of hands-on learning for undergraduates and realize benefits from my association with these researchers, I have been able to find ways to integrate them in nearly all aspects of my roles of teaching, research, and service. I also work in a climate that is collegial and conducive to a shared sense of responsibility for guiding undergraduates.

Faculty members have many opportunities to help students build the foundation skills to undertake research and to also supervise the research. A primary responsibility is for a teacher to introduce students to the nature, history, and methods of a discipline. For faculty looking for opportunities to stimulate undergraduate research and creative endeavors, I offer the following checklist.

How Does the Course Design Lay the Groundwork for Undergraduate Research?

In the assigned readings, are there original works from research journals, as opposed to exclusive reliance on textbooks?

Is some attention paid to the rhetoric employed in these articles— the structure, format, peer-review process, and semantics of the discipline?

In addition to "results," is there discussion of the research process itself?

Are students given the analytical tools to critique pieces of scholarship in the discipline? Besides methods, are ethical issues highlighted?

Do course assignments include systematic library research, an annotated bibliography, or a review of literature?

Are class periods structured in such a way that students can "co-construct" their understanding of the literature they are reading?

Do students have an opportunity to participate in a simulation in which data are collected and analyzed?

Do students have an opportunity to participate in an original research project in which data are collected and analyzed?

Do students have an opportunity to design a research project? Carry it to completion?

Will original student scholarship be "published" (on the class Web site, for example) or presented as part of the course?

How Might Students Help in the Development of Courses?

Are students employed to assist the instructor in searching the literature for course materials?

Are students employed to assist the instructor in carrying out course assessment?

To the extent that students assist with these activities, is care taken to select students with the greatest potential for growth? Is the work handled in a developmental way so that students gain maximum benefit from the experience?

Do students have opportunities to apply creative and technical skills in producing original graphic or computer-based material for the course?

Is accommodation made so that students can "present" or publish the contributions they have made to the course?

How does a faculty member find talented students?

Is the faculty member alert to potential researchers?

Once talent is spotted, can the faculty member point these students toward appropriate avenues to develop their talent such as employment with colleagues, the honors program, undergraduate research funds, and celebrations of undergraduate researchers?

Has the faculty member made his or her research interests known to a centralized register on campus that maintains a database for prospective student researchers?

How Can Undergraduates Be Involved in Faculty Research?

Are undergraduates involved in the faculty member's research? Is the work treated as an apprenticeship, with tasks graded in level of responsibility?

Are graduate and undergraduate students brought together in a collaborative atmosphere where the entire research enterprise is the focus of guided discussion? Is the undergraduate given increasingly complex tasks beyond washing test tubes?

In writing grants, are undergraduate research assistants written into the budget? In writing National Science Foundation grants, is a Research Experiences for Undergraduates supplement requested (available at http://www.nsf.gov/search97cgi/vtopic)?

Is the faculty member aware of and does he or she take advantage of any campus programs that provide funds to support undergraduate research?

Do students participate in data analysis, write-up, presentation, and publication?

Do undergraduates travel to conferences with the faculty mentor? Are they socialized into the profession or discipline?

Are students involved in consulting done by the faculty member?

What Can a Faculty Member Do as a University Citizen?

Are there opportunities to participate in campuswide curricular reform efforts that promote active engagement, interdisciplinary perspectives, freshman seminars, senior theses, or capstone experiences?

Are there opportunities to lend support to or participate in the development of the honors or undergraduate research programs, an undergraduate research grants fund, the undergraduate "scholar's day," or similar recognition and display of student work?

Is there scope for the faculty member to lobby to strengthen requirements for the major to include research methods and research experience components?

Has the faculty member read the Boyer Commission report or become familiar with the goals of the Reinvention Center (http://www.sunysb.edu/reinventioncenter)?

Does the faculty member represent the institution at state, regional, and national undergraduate research conferences?

Has the faculty member joined the National Conferences on Undergraduate Research (http://www.ncur.org), the Council on Undergraduate Research (http://www.cur.org), or the National Collegiate Honors Council (http://www.nchchonors.org)? Are students informed and sponsored to attend and present at these venues?

Conclusion

Fundamentally, the challenge of incorporating undergraduates into one's scholarly or professional work is through creative fragmentation of the tasks at hand. Even a humanist, normally the most solitary of scholars, can redefine work in ways that allow for collaboration.

I argue that each faculty member can find ways to get involved in fostering and mentoring undergraduate research. From my own experiences, it is a transformative process for professor and student, one worthy of investment.

References

Andrew, M. "Edutainment in Anthropology: A Double-Edged Sword." *Teaching Anthropology Newsletter,* Fall 1999-Spring 2000, *35–36,* 2–4.

Boyer, E. L. *Scholarship Reconsidered: Priorities of the Professoriate.* Princeton, N.J.: Carnegie Foundation for the Advancement of Teaching, Princeton University Press, 1990.

Boyer Commission on Educating Undergraduates in the Research University. *Reinventing Undergraduate Education: A Blueprint for America's Research Universities.* State University of New York–Stony Brook, 1998.

Emmet, J. "The Paradox of Infanticide." Unpublished honors senior thesis, Utah State University, 2001.

Lancy, D. F., and Call, D. *The Kin Game.* Modules in Teaching Anthropology #5. Washington, D.C.: American Anthropological Association, 1998.

Lancy, D. F., and others. "Whose Mummy Is It?" [http://www.egyptinteractive.com/whose_mummy/whose_main.htm]. 2000.

DAVID F. LANCY, *professor of anthropology at Utah State University, was named the Utah Professor of the Year in 2001 by the Carnegie Foundation and CASE. He believes the award was due primarily to his innovative use of technology in teaching and his mentorship of undergraduates.*

INDEX

Back Issue/Subscription Order Form

Copy or detach and send to:
Jossey-Bass, A Wiley Company, 989 Market Street, San Francisco CA 94103-1741

Call or fax toll-free: Phone 888-378-2537 6:30AM – 3PM PST; Fax 888-481-2665

Back Issues: Please send me the following issues at $27 each
(Important: please include ISBN number with your order.)

_____

_____

_____

$ _____   Total for single issues

$ _____   SHIPPING CHARGES: SURFACE   Domestic Canadian

	First Item	$5.00	$6.00
	Each Add'l Item	$3.00	$1.50

For next-day and second-day delivery rates, call the number listed above.

Subscriptions   Please __ start __ renew my subscription to *New Directions for Teaching and Learning* for the year 2___ at the following rate:

U.S.	__ Individual $70	__ Institutional $145
Canada	__ Individual $70	__ Institutional $185
All Others	__ Individual $94	__ Institutional $219
Online Subscription		__ Institutional $145

**For more information about online subscriptions visit
www.interscience.wiley.com**

$ _____   Total single issues and subscriptions (Add appropriate sales tax for your state for single issue orders. No sales tax for U.S. subscriptions. Canadian residents, add GST for subscriptions and single issues.)

__Payment enclosed (U.S. check or money order only)
__VISA __ MC __ AmEx __ Discover Card #_____ Exp. Date _____

Signature _____ Day Phone _____
__ Bill Me (U.S. institutional orders only. Purchase order required.)

Purchase order # _____
Federal Tax ID13559302   **GST 89102 8052**

Name _____

Address _____

_____

Phone _____ E-mail _____

For more information about Jossey-Bass, visit our Web site at www.josseybass.com

PROMOTION CODE ND03

TL88   **Fresh Approaches to the Evaluation of Teaching**
        Christopher Knapper, Patricia Cranton
        Describes a number of alternative approaches, including interpretive and
        critical evaluation, use of teaching portfolios and teaching awards,
        performance indicators and learning outcomes, technology-mediated
        evaluation systems, and the role of teacher accreditation and teaching
        scholarship in instructional evaluation.
        ISBN: 0-7879-5789-5

TL87   **Techniques and Strategies for Interpreting Student Evaluations**
        Karron G. Lewis
        Focuses on all phases of the student rating process—from data-gathering
        methods to presentation of results. Topics include methods of encouraging
        meaningful evaluations, mid-semester feedback, uses of quality teams and
        focus groups, and creating questions that target individual faculty needs and
        interest.
        ISBN: 0-7879-5789-5

TL86   **Scholarship Revisited: Perspectives on the Scholarship of Teaching**
        Carolin Kreber
        Presents the outcomes of a Delphi Study conducted by an international
        panel of academics working in faculty evaluation scholarship and
        postsecondary teaching and learning. Identifies the important components of
        scholarship of teaching, defines its characteristics and outcomes, and
        explores its most pressing issues.
        ISBN: 0-7879-5447-0

TL85   **Beyond Teaching to Mentoring**
        Alice G. Reinarz, Eric R. White
        Offers guidelines to optimizing student learning through classroom activities
        as well as peer, faculty, and professional mentoring. Addresses mentoring
        techniques in technical training, undergraduate business, science, and liberal
        arts studies, health professions, international study, and interdisciplinary
        work.
        ISBN: 0-7879-5617-1

TL84   **Principles of Effective Teaching in the Online Classroom**
        Renée E. Weiss, Dave S. Knowlton, Bruce W. Speck
        Discusses structuring the online course, utilizing resources from the World
        Wide Web and using other electronic tools and technology to enhance
        classroom efficiency. Addresses challenges unique to the online classroom
        community, including successful communication strategies, performance
        evaluation, academic integrity, and accessibility for disabled students.
        ISBN: 0-7879-5615-5

TL83   **Evaluating Teaching in Higher Education: A Vision for the Future**
        Katherine E. Ryan
        Analyzes the strengths and weaknesses of current approaches to evaluating
        teaching and recommends practical strategies for improving current
        evaluation methods and developing new ones. Provides an overview of new
        techniques such as peer evaluations, portfolios, and student ratings of
        instructors and technologies.
        ISBN: 0-7879-5448-9

TL70 **Approaches to Teaching Non-Native English Speakers Across the Curriculum**
David L. Sigsbee, Bruce W. Speck, Bruce Maylath
Provides strategies that help students who are non-native users of English improve their writing and speaking skills in content-area courses. Considers the points of view of the students themselves and discusses their differing levels of intent about becoming proficient in English writing and speaking.
ISBN: 0-7879-9860-5

TL69 **Writing to Learn: Strategies for Assigning and Responding to Writing Across the Disciplines**
Mary Deane Sorcinelli, Peter Elbow
Presents strategies and philosophies about the way writing is learned, both in the context of a discipline and as an independent skill. Focusing primarily on the best ways to give feedback about written work, the authors describe a host of alternatives that have a solid foundation in research.
ISBN: 0-7879-9859-1

TL68 **Bringing Problem-Based Learning to Higher Education: Theory and Practice**
LuAnn Wilkerson, Wim H. Gijselaers
Describes the basics of problem-based learning, along with the variables that affect its success. Provides examples of its application in a wide range of disciplines, including medicine, business, education, engineering, mathematics, and the sciences.
ISBN: 0-7879-9934-2

TL67 **Using Active Learning in College Classes: A Range of Options for Faculty**
Tracey E. Sutherland, Charles C. Bonwell
Examines the use of active learning in higher education and describes the concept of the active learning continuum, tying various practical examples of active learning to that concept.
ISBN: 0-7879-9933-4

TL66 **Ethical Dimensions of College and University Teaching: Understanding and Honoring the Special Relationship Between Teachers and Students**
Linc Fisch
Illustrates that responsibility to students is directly related to the understanding of one's ethical self, and that the first step in establishing that ethical identity is self-reflection. Details the transformation of structures and attitudes that ethical teaching fosters.
ISBN: 0-7879-9910-5

TL65 **Honoring Exemplary Teaching**
Marilla D. Svinicki, Robert J. Menges
Describes programs for faculty recognition in a variety of settings and with varying purposes. Reviews research relevant to selection criteria, and offers guidelines for planning and implementing effective programs.
ISBN: 0-7879-9979-2

NEW DIRECTIONS FOR TEACHING AND LEARNING IS NOW AVAILABLE ONLINE AT WILEY INTERSCIENCE

What is Wiley InterScience?

Wiley InterScience is the dynamic online content service from John Wiley & Sons delivering the full text of over 300 leading scientific, technical, medical, and professional journals, plus major reference works, the acclaimed Current Protocols laboratory manuals, and even the full text of select Wiley print books online.

What are some special features of Wiley InterScience?

Wiley Interscience Alerts is a service that delivers table of contents via e-mail for any journal available on Wiley InterScience as soon as a new issue is published online.

EarlyView is Wiley's exclusive service presenting individual articles online as soon as they are ready, even before the release of the compiled print issue. These articles are complete, peer-reviewed, and citable.

CrossRef is the innovative multi-publisher reference linking system enabling readers to move seamlessly from a reference in a journal article to the cited publication, typically located on a different server and published by a different publisher.

How can I access Wiley InterScience?

Visit http://www.interscience.wiley.com.

Guest Users can browse Wiley InterScience for unrestricted access to journal tables of contents and article abstracts, or use the powerful search engine.

Registered Users are provided with a *Personal Home Page* to store and manage customized alerts, searches, and links to favorite journals and articles. Additionally, Registered Users can view free online sample issues and preview selected material from major reference works.

Licensed Customers are entitled to access full-text journal articles in PDF, with select journals also offering full-text HTML.

How do I become an Authorized User?

Authorized Users are individuals authorized by a paying Customer to have access to the journals in Wiley InterScience. For example, a university that subscribes to Wiley journals is considered to be the Customer.

Faculty, staff and students authorized by the university to have access to those journals in Wiley InterScience are Authorized Users. Users should contact their library for information on which Wiley journals they have access to in Wiley InterScience.

United States Postal Service

Statement of Ownership, Management, and Circulation

1 Publication Title	2 Publication Number	13 Filing Date
New Directions For Teaching And Learning	0 2 7 1 - 0 6 3	9/26/02

4. Issue Frequency	5 Number of Issues Published Annually	6. Annual Subscription Price
Quarterly	4	$70.00 Individual $145.00 Institution

7. Complete Mailing Address of Known Office of Publication (Not printer) (Street, city, county, state, and ZIP+4)

989 Market Street
San Francisco, CA 94103-1741
San Francisco County

Contact Person
Joe Schuman
Telephone
415 782 3232

8. Complete Mailing Address of Headquarters or General Business Office of Publisher (Not printer)

Same as above

9. Full Names and Complete Mailing Addresses of Publisher, Editor, and Managing Editor (Do not leave blank)

Publisher (Name and complete mailing address)

Jossey-Bass, A Wiley Company
Above Address

Editor (Name and complete mailing address)

Marilla D. Svinicki
Center For Teaching Effectiveness/Univ of Austin
Main Bldg. 2200
Austin, TX 78712-111

Managing Editor (Name and complete mailing address)

None

10. Owner (Do not leave blank. If the publication is owned by a corporation, give the name and address of the corporation immediately followed by the names and addresses of all stockholders owning or holding 1 percent or more of the total amount of stock. If not owned by a corporation, give the names and addresses of the individual owners. If owned by a partnership or other unincorporated firm, give its name and address as well as those of each individual owner. If the publication is published by a nonprofit organization, give its name and address.)

Full Name	Complete Mailing Address
John Wiley & Sons Inc.	111 River Street Hoboken, NJ 07030

11. Known Bondholders, Mortgagees, and Other Security Holders Owning or Holding 1 Percent or More of Total Amount of Bonds, Mortgages, or Other Securities. If none, check box.   ☐ None

Full Name	Complete Mailing Address
Same as Above	Same As Above

12. Tax Status. (For completion by nonprofit organizations authorized to mail at nonprofit rates) (Check one)
The purpose, function, and nonprofit status of this organization and the exempt status for federal income tax purposes:
☐ Has Not Changed During Preceding 12 Months
☐ Has Changed During Preceding 12 Months (Publisher must submit explanation of change with this statement)

PS Form 3526, October 1999   (See Instructions on Reverse)

---

13 Publication Title	14 Issue Date for Circulation Data Below
New Directions For Teaching And Learning	Summer 2002

15	Extent and Nature of Circulation	Average No. Copies Each Issue During Preceding 12 Months	No. Copies of Single Issue Published Nearest to Filing Date
a.	Total Number of Copies (Net press run)	1,595	1,620
b. Paid and/or Requested Circulation	(1) Paid/Requested Outside-County Mail Subscriptions Stated on Form 3541 (Include advertiser's proof and exchange copies)	923	919
	(2) Paid In-County Subscriptions Stated on Form 3541 (Include advertiser's proof and exchange copies)	0	0
	(3) Sales Through Dealers and Carriers, Street Vendors, Counter Sales, and Other Non-USPS Paid Distribution	0	0
	(4) Other Classes Mailed Through the USPS	0	0
c.	Total Paid and/or Requested Circulation (Sum of 15b. (1), (2),(3),and (4))	923	919
d. Free Distribution by Mail (Samples, compliment ary, and other free)	(1) Outside-County as Stated on Form 3541	0	0
	(2) In-County as Stated on Form 3541	0	0
	(3) Other Classes Mailed Through the USPS	1	1
e.	Free Distribution Outside the Mail (Carriers or other means)	39	39
f.	Total Free Distribution (Sum of 15d. and 15e.)	40	40
g.	Total Distribution (Sum of 15c. and 15f)	963	959
h.	Copies not Distributed	632	661
i.	Total (Sum of 15g. and h.)	1,595	1,620
j.	Percent Paid and/or Requested Circulation (15c. divided by 15g. times 100)	96%	96%

16. Publication of Statement of Ownership
☐ Publication required. Will be printed in the Winter 2002 issue of this publication.   ☐ Publication not required.

17. Signature and Title of Editor, Publisher, Business Manager, or Owner   Susan E. Lewis
Susan E. Lewis   VP & Publisher - Periodicals   Date 9/26/02

I certify that all information furnished on this form is true and complete. I understand that anyone who furnishes false or misleading information on this form or who omits material or information requested on the form may be subject to criminal sanctions (including fines and imprisonment) and/or civil sanctions (including civil penalties).

Instructions to Publishers

1. Complete and file one copy of this form with your postmaster annually on or before October 1. Keep a copy of the completed form for your records.

2. In cases where the stockholder or security holder is a trustee, include in items 10 and 11 the name of the person or corporation for whom the trustee is acting. Also include the names and addresses of individuals who are stockholders who own or hold 1 percent or more of the total amount of bonds, mortgages, or other securities of the publishing corporation. In item 11, if none, check the box. Use blank sheets if more space is required.

3. Be sure to furnish all circulation information called for in item 15. Free circulation must be shown in items 15d, e, and f.

4. Item 15h., Copies not Distributed, must include (1) newsstand copies originally stated on Form 3541, and returned to the publisher, (2) estimated returns from news agents, and (3), copies for office use, leftovers, spoiled, and all other copies not distributed.

5. If the publication had Periodicals authorization as a general or requester publication, this Statement of Ownership, Management, and Circulation must be published; it must be printed in any issue in October or, if the publication is not published during October, the first issue printed after October.

6. In item 16, indicate the date of the issue in which this Statement of Ownership will be published.

7. Item 17 must be signed.

Failure to file or publish a statement of ownership may lead to suspension of Periodicals authorization.

PS Form 3526, October 1999 (Reverse)